fe·ral | ˈfer-əl |
adjective

1. The way you lead when you care too much to play it safe. Your intensity isn't a liability, it's Signal.

Your questions cut deeper than comfort allows. You see what's coming three steps before anyone asks.

You've been called too direct, too early, too much, too fast, too intense, too curious, too honest, *too everything.*

You didn't break the mold. You never meant to fit it.

2. The state where impostor syndrome gets fired, perfectionism loses its grip, and you stop auditioning for approval.

FERAL
GUIDESHIP

A FIELD GUIDE FOR LEADERS & TEAMS

LINDA CLARK

FERAL GUIDESHIP
Copyright © 2025 by Linda Clark
All rights reserved.

www.feralguideship.com
www.linda-clark.com

Published by Curiosetti Ink
Murphy, North Carolina

No part of this book may be reproduced or distributed in any form or by any means without the prior permission of the publisher or author. Requests for permission should be directed to connect@linda-clark.com.

Neither the publisher nor the author is engaged in rendering legal or other professional services through this book. If expert assistance is required, the services of appropriate professionals should be sought. The publisher and the author shall have neither liability nor responsibility to any person or entity with respect to any loss or damage caused directly or indirectly by the information in this publication.

The Curiosetti Method™, VERGE Coaching Model™, and Feral Guideship™ are pending trademarks of Linda Clark and Linda Clark Consulting LLC.

ISBN: 979-8-218-75098-5 (Print)
ISBN: 979-8-218-75099-2 (eBook)
Library of Congress Control Number: 2025921961

Ethics and Authorship Statement
Feral Guideship is built from lived experience, professional practice, and the author's original frameworks and voice. Every idea, method, and line of this book was conceived and written by Linda Clark. AI tools such as ChatGPT and Claude were used only for editing support, refining rhythm, clarity, and consistency under the author's full direction and supervision. All creative decisions, language, and intellectual property remain solely the work of the author.

Original cover concept by NikkiJo Fair
Printed in the United States of America
First Edition

For my husband, Bob, who had no idea what feral *really* meant when he signed up. Twenty-two years in, thank you for staying curious about where the trail leads.

For my mother, who chose the straighter path and somehow raised wild thinkers and good goblins while keeping her blood pressure stable. That's no small miracle.

For the Guides who found me when I was still wearing the masks of compliance and approval: teachers, mentors, beautiful misfits, and fellow pathfinders who brought flashlights, pointed toward possibility, and never once suggested I turn back.

And for every single one of you told to tone it down, dial it back, be reasonable. To wait your turn, dim your light, and smile on command.

That box they offered you? It's not safety. It's suffocation.

I'm glad you said no.
I'm glad you're still here.
I'm glad you know it matters.

With so much love,
this one is for you.

Expedition Map

The Invitation

PREFACE
For The Curious Who Came This Far — 3

INTRODUCTION
An Orientation for The Curious — 7

The Emergence

CHAPTER 1
The Trust Recession — 15
Perspective · Reality · Consequence

CHAPTER 2
The Compass for The Curious — 29
The Method · Ecosystemic Leadership

CHAPTER 3
The Audacity of Identity — 45
Experience · Presence · Originality

CHAPTER 4
The Ethos of Reclamation — 61
Agency · Purpose · Integrity

CHAPTER 5
The Mycelia of Inclusion — 79
Belonging · Community · Sustainability

The Confluence

CHAPTER 6
The Collective Strategic Mind — 97
Signal Intelligence for Strategy and Teams

CHAPTER 7
The Practice of Vision — 113
Generative Vision for Purpose and Alignment

CHAPTER 8
The Navigation Problem — 127
Relational Gravity for Trust and Belonging

CHAPTER 9
The Spark of Momentum — 143
Courage and Creative Instigation

Expedition Map

The Confluence

CHAPTER 10
The Gravity of Wholeness — 161
The Living System of Influence and Impact

CHAPTER 11
The Return to Center — 175
The Resonance of Feral Guideship

Base Camp

About the Author — 187

Choose Your Own Adventure — 191
Guided Reading Trails by Topic

The Individual
- Trust in Uncertain Times — 191
- Integrity and Alignment — 191
- Strategic Curiosity — 191
- Courage, Creativity, and Innovation — 192
- Hope and Renewal — 192
- Identity and Authentic Leadership — 192

The Team
- Signal and Clarity in Communication — 192
- Collaboration and Collective Intelligence — 193
- Conflict and Restoration — 193
- Being Trustworthy — 193
- Decision Making — 193
- Accountability and Follow Through — 193

The Culture
- Belonging and Inclusion — 194
- Systems Thinking — 194
- Adaptability and Change — 194
- Purpose and Regeneration — 194
- Purpose and Legacy — 194

The Invitation
Where Guides Gather

For the Curious Who Came This Far

PREFACE

Well, well, well. Look what the forest dragged in.

If you've ever been told you're too much, too direct, too early, too intense, this stump is for you. Sit. Let the moss cushion you. You belong here.

For years, I tried to squeeze myself into descriptions, checklists, and boxes to play the Game of Professionalism and Career Success. HR policies, board meetings, leadership retreats where the air reeked of lemon-scented flip charts and false enthusiasm. Every time I molded myself into a softer version, I disappeared a little more.

I'd crack a joke that cut too deep, or name the thing everyone else danced around, and get... *the look*. You know the one. The one that says: Please. Tone it down. Be 90% less...you.

Maybe you've gotten that look, too.

What I didn't know then? The very parts of me they wanted toned down were exactly what could cut through nonsense and guide people somewhere better. Humor sharp enough to cut through the tension of conflict and discomfort. Curiosity that wouldn't stop asking why until it reached something true. The willingness to move, decide, and iterate while others waited for perfect conditions that would never come.

Here's what that pressure taught me: Every time they asked me to shrink, I got sharper. Every time they begged me to tone it down, I understood better how this feral spirit works. Every time they labeled me as *too much*, I started to suspect that maybe... *too much* was exactly the right dose.

That tension? That's where this method was born. Not from ease. Not from perfect mentorship, but from **resistance**. From watching systems reject the very ingenuity they claimed to value, then seeing what happened when people like us kept showing up anyway.

I spent fifteen years cheerfully climbing the ladder, learning the corporate language, nodding in all the right places, while constantly being told I was too direct, too intense, too impatient. Then one day, a leader looked at me and saw something completely different.

He watched me dismantle systems that weren't working, spot problems everyone else tiptoed around, and care more about real outcomes than political consequences. He grasped something most didn't. Silence didn't feel safe to me. It felt like betrayal. Like watching rot spread while everyone pretended the smell was normal.

The miracle wasn't that he saw me. It's that he **wanted** to be challenged. I questioned his decisions, he engaged back. I named what felt hollow. Instead of managing me down, he leaned in and asked for more. Demanded it, really.

Where others saw friction, he saw pattern recognition. Where they saw a problem to coach away, he saw perception that wouldn't quit. One day, he pulled me aside and said something that still runs electric through me: "You know this thing you do? It's *inevitable*."

Inevitable. Do you know what that word does to someone who's spent their whole life being told to take it down a notch?

He let my inquisitive and irreverent nature grow, not out of neglect, but trust. Enough structure to hold it, enough care to keep it reaching. He watered what mattered and trusted the rest to find its own way to the light.

That's the generative part of Guideship. You don't mold someone into a better version of yourself. You create the space where more capacity emerges.

That's how I learned to recognize other Guides in the wild. Not the ones with shiny titles or branded toolkits, but the ones you *must* notice. The ones who move toward tension with clarity instead of avoidance. The ones who quietly change an entire perspective by refusing to perform the usual dance.

Guideship wasn't something I invented. It was something I recognized. Leaders who weren't performing leadership theater but guiding in real time. People who didn't wait for readiness but stepped forward anyway. People who understood that culture doesn't shift by decree. It shifts when someone crosses first, and others follow.

For nearly thirty years, I've watched systems break brilliant, feral people by shoving them into sanitized molds. I've shoved, and been shoved.

I've also watched what happens when those same people reclaim their signal and take their seat at the fire. That's where the real work begins.

This book works with **who you are**. Not who you should be. Not the corporate cutout version. You, with your humor, tenderness, expertise, originality, and all those unique skills, quirks, and edges you've been told to... manage. We're bringing all of it into the rooms that need it most.

You're here because you know the old models are cracked. Because you've been holding your breath, waiting for something more alive. Because you're one of **The Curious**, and you're ready to move.

Let's set a course.

An Orientation for The Curious

INTRODUCTION

You walk into rooms where decisions get made, and your body knows before your brain catches up. The calculation starts: How much of myself can I bring without paying for it later? How much truth can this room hold? How much of my brain is welcome here?

You're done with leadership as an amateur production of control with pretty words. The glossy transformation promises. The endless meetings where everyone performs competence while real problems rot in the corners. You know there's a better way because you've been in the room when someone drops the script and speaks with their full voice, and we all think, "Well...finally someone said it."

You've memorized enough frameworks. You've deployed them on command. You know what manuals do, they pile instructions on your desk and call it progress. I lovingly call them guilt binders. We won't use them, but we won't throw them away either.

This book does something else entirely.

This is about remembering how to guide with your complete self: your pattern recognition that others dismiss as "too early," your willingness to name what everyone else tiptoes around, your refusal to pretend that broken systems just need better management.

This is for the explorers. The Curious. The ones who ask better questions than they give answers, who create space for others to grow alongside them, who understand that the best leadership happens when people feel safe enough to think out loud.

The Territory We're Mapping

The Curiosetti Method integrates three elements: **Seeds of Potential**, the living capacities that already exist within you; **Guideship**, the adaptive stance that lets you move fluidly between leading, managing, and following as each moment requires; and **Signal**, how your intention travels through culture and becomes impact others can perceive, receive, and believe.

Chapters 1 through 5, are your base camp. This is where the journey begins. Why traditional leadership development has become an elaborate game of dress-up where everyone looks the part, but nobody remembers how to guide. The Seeds of Potential that live within you, constellations of capacity waiting to be reclaimed.

What Guideship looks like when it's lived instead of performed, how it moves differently than the management rituals most organizations mistake for leadership, and why cultures are starving for people who can navigate complexity with wisdom instead of whatever buzzword is trending this quarter.

And Signal, the resonance of your presence that travels far beyond any single interaction. How your intention transforms into impact, how trust builds or crumbles through countless small choices, and how authentic leadership creates ripple effects that strengthen entire systems rather than polishing individual reputations.

This section gives you everything you need to navigate what comes next. You'll learn to read the landscape, understand your own capacities, and work with tools that will serve you across any leadership challenge you encounter.

The Wilderness Awaits

After base camp comes the real adventure. The rest of this book opens into a wilderness of modern leadership challenges, each one a territory worth exploring: Building unshakeable trust in environments that breed suspicion. Creating genuine belonging in cultures that mistake diversity initiatives for inclusion. Driving innovation when risk has been regulated into extinction.

Navigating strategy when the old playbooks can't touch the complexity you're facing. Making decisions with incomplete information and high stakes. Recovering from mistakes without losing credibility or momentum. Delivering outcomes that matter instead of metrics that shine in quarterly reviews and tarnish the minute folks leave the room.

The territories connect, but you don't need to traverse them in order. Someone wrestling with team dynamics after a major reorganization will head different directions than someone building an innovative culture in a compliance-conditioned environment. An executive recovering from a public failure will explore different ground than a manager trying to influence up in an organization that doesn't value their perspective.

Sometimes you just want a guided day trip, a focused path for a specific issue or theme. You'll find those in the Choose Your Own Adventure section (p. 195) and listed in the Table of Contents. Each route offers a quick way to navigate directly to the ideas that fit your current terrain, whether you're rebuilding trust, clarifying direction, or recalibrating culture.

Find a Signal Check at the end of each chapter with anchoring questions for you or the adventure of someone you're mentoring, teams committed to exploration, and the full expedition of asking culture changing questions. Come back to those to anchor in the work and remain committed.

Follow what calls to you. Dive deep where you need depth. Return to foundational concepts when you want to see them through fresh eyes.

What You're Signing Up For

You're not here to "optimize your influence" or learn better people management techniques. Those are small games for people who think leadership is about control.

What you're after is bigger: the ability to guide with your full self. Your intuition, your expertise, your experience. To build cultures where the smartest people don't have to perform stupidity to fit in. To create space where curiosity and courage don't have to wait for permission from three approval layers, the steering committee, and what's-her-name from down the hall with an opinion about… everything.

You want to stop translating yourself into corporate-speak before you open your mouth. You're done watching promising ideas suffocate while urgent problems metastasize. No one wants to disrupt the illusion of alignment.

Organizations that figure this out first won't just win. They'll operate in a different relationship with reality. They'll keep the talent others lose because brilliant people can smell the difference between a culture that wants their compliance and one that wants their intelligence.

They'll spot problems before they become crises. Pattern recognition doesn't need a task force to give it permission to notice. They'll adapt while others are still arguing about the org chart.

You'll measure your progress differently too. Not in performance reviews or promotion timelines, but in how you show up. The confidence that replaces the calculation. The clarity that replaces the scripts. The knowing, when you walk into any room, that you belong there.

Success looks like being yourself and watching that create space for everyone else to do the same.

How to Navigate This Wilderness

Start by building your foundation. Read Section 1 straight through. Get your compass, understand the landscape, establish your base camp. After that, trust your instincts about what you need when you need it.

Each section in the wilderness stands on its own while contributing to something larger: leadership that regenerates instead of depletes, cultures rooted in genuine human discernment instead of performance anxiety, organizations that bend without breaking because they're built on trust instead of control.

Skip around. Circle back. Dive deep where your curiosity leads. This book is designed to be lived with, not read once. The challenges you face next year will send you to different chapters than the ones calling to you today. Your growing mastery will reveal new layers in what you thought you already understood.

The only rule is honesty. With yourself, with your team, with the systems you're trying to change. Exploration doesn't thrive on pretense. It needs truth the way plants need sunlight.

Why This Matters More Than You Think

The ground is shifting under our feet economically, politically, technologically, culturally. Leaders who keep trying to control their way through uncertainty will exhaust themselves and everyone around them. Organizations that mistake compliance for competence will discover how fragile their foundations are when the next wave hits.

This moment cracks everything wide open.

The future belongs to guides. People who can read patterns others miss, ask questions others avoid, and create the conditions where insight surfaces and solutions emerge. They trust the people around them enough to let the right answers find their way into the light.

Evolution and transformation move faster than planning cycles can track. Guides know this and stay ready.

You already carry everything you need for this work. The curiosity they told you was disruptive. The intensity they asked you to tone down. The questions that made people uncomfortable. The pattern recognition that arrived too early for everyone else's timeline. The refusal to nod along when something doesn't add up.

Your leadership operating systems runs on these features. This moment in time demands exactly what you've got.

While others are still trying to optimize their way through complexity, you'll be navigating it. While they're waiting for the perfect strategy, you'll be learning in real time. While they're *managing the optics*, you'll be building trust that lets teams move fast without breaking.

This is your moment. You're willing to show up as yourself and figure it out as you go.

Welcome to the Real Work

So welcome to the wilderness, explorer. Section 1 will orient you and equip you with everything you need to navigate what lies ahead. After that, the territory is rich with challenges that matter, problems worth solving, and opportunities to create the kinds of cultures where feral intelligence can flourish instead of endure.

You bring strengths worth recognizing. Go all in on them. Grow them as you move through this territory, then build the conditions where others can do the same.

You'll stumble. You'll misread situations. You'll try something bold and watch it land flat. That's not failure. That's how guides learn to read new terrain.

The difference is, you'll keep moving anyway.

The old paths are disappearing. Might as well forge new ones that lead somewhere worth going.

Ready to remember what you're capable of when you stop performing leadership and start living it? Ready to build the kinds of cultures where people bring their full selves because hiding costs too much?

Let's find out.

The Emergence

The Intentional Practice of Guideship

One

The Trust Recession

Perspective · Reality · Consequence

Your phone buzzes. Again. Slack, email, calendar, text. All screaming urgency. By noon, you've triaged forty-two crises and advanced nothing that will matter six months from now. Congratulations. You spent your best thinking hours being a highly responsive human traffic cone.

This is what leadership has become. **Urgency wearing importance like a fake ID.** Every notification promises breakthrough. Every meeting promises clarity. Instead, you get the strategy everyone's too scared to execute, the hire trapped in approval purgatory, and the decision that's been "almost ready" for three quarters while the actual problem grows teeth.

You've perfected this dance. Smoothed every edge off your language so it won't startle anyone in the approval chain. Watched your smartest colleague perform confusion in a meeting because clarity would expose how long leadership has been wrong. Spent Wednesday wordsmithing a deck that says nothing because saying something might require someone to act.

The system rewards this. It promotes people who've mastered the performance. It calls your instincts "premature" and your pattern recognition "not data-driven enough." It asks you to be 60% less yourself and wonders why innovation feels like pushing a boulder uphill in flip-flops.

But here's what they missed while they were domesticating you: **you were never the problem.**

Well... mostly.

Why Feral? Why Guideship? Why Now?

The data is boring in its consistency. Gallup, McKinsey, DDI, pick your source. They all say the same thing: organizations need innovation, creative problem-solving, initiative, real connection. Not as aspirations. As conditions for success.

Yet what shows up instead is hesitation, recycled answers, and cultures that freeze when the stakes climb. The Age of Obedience has passed.

The problem isn't talent or effort. It's that cultures have been **domesticated** into compliance, perfection, and performance theater.

Feral is a reclamation. We were all feral once. That capacity still lives in leaders, in teams, and in every person who wants to create, risk, and recover. Feral restores what's been buried so cultures can generate ideas, strengthen connection, and deliver results.

When I first mentioned feral in the same sentence as talent, a very-buttoned-up (VBU) professional gasped, "You mean, like naked in the WOODS?" Now, I had no idea about their social life before that moment, but hey, maybe... we should be friends! And no, that's not what I meant. At all.

Feral is a **rewilded posture of leadership** that treats resilience and feedback as assets, honors lived experience as knowledge and embodies originality rather than imitation. A state of self-awareness and trust where a person moves with confidence in their experience and expertise.

It is the stance of a leader who claims contributions and success without apology, acknowledges mistakes with faith in their ability to recover and grow, and resists the grip of impostor syndrome, perfectionism, and self-doubt.

Whew. That last part? I work on it... a lot.

But *you know that.*

You see the fracture lines before anyone else admits there's a crack. You ask the question that makes the room go silent because it's the one everyone's been avoiding. You connect what's happening now to what will break later, You connect what's happening now to what will break later. People mistake attention for prophecy.

The instinct they called "jumping to conclusions." The honesty they labeled "not a team player." The impatience with bureaucratic theater when real problems need solving. The willingness to say the true thing instead of the safe thing. Those aren't character flaws to manage. Those are survival skills for organizations that want to make it through what's coming.

The "too much" you've always been is exactly what this moment is starving for.

You're here because you're done translating yourself into corporate before you speak. You've watched too many brilliant people learn to perform confusion, so they don't threaten anyone's comfort. You've watched imagination get suffocated by process and wondered if you were the only one who noticed.

You're not. I see you. **I am you.** And we're done pretending the emperor's new clothes look great when we can all see he's naked and freezing.

Perfectionism Is Killing Thought

Perfectionism whispers the most seductive lie: if you get it flawless, no one can fault you. Mistake-free equals safe. The logic feels airtight until you watch what it does to intelligence, creativity, and the capacity to move when stakes climb.

Perfect doesn't build trust. **It builds paralysis.** Flaws hide under glossy formatting while creative capacity that could solve real problems burns out at midnight perfecting slides. Weekends vanish into pitches that crumble at the first hard question. Teams rehearse certainty instead of creating anything worth being certain about.

Watch what perfectionism does to strategic thinking. Real strategy requires experimentation, rapid learning, messy iteration. Perfection demands certainty before action. Strategy becomes slideware. Innovation becomes performance. The nerve to say "Let's try this and see what we learn" gets buried under endless rehearsal.

The project that died because it couldn't get approval until every variable was controlled. The idea that withered while legal, compliance, and three committees weighed in on what was meant to be a quick experiment. The breakthrough that never happened because someone needed 100% certainty before they'd allow anyone to find out.

And then there's innovation performance. Leaders build labs, run hackathons, scatter beanbags and sticky notes across windowless rooms. They talk disruption and future-proofing. But prototypes never see funding. Post-its never leave the wall. Labs never touch real problems customers face.

Performance is neat and comfortable. Real innovation is messy and uncertain. It requires confidence that says, **"I don't know if this will work, but I trust my ability to find out."**

Guess which one gets funded?

The part that would be funny if it weren't so expensive? Organizations run a **wine tasting for bad ideas.** "Ooh, I'm getting notes of synergy, with a long compliance finish." Everyone swirls the talking points, sniffs risk from a safe distance, and says, "I detect a hint of courage," while never swallowing it.

If you laughed, you've been in that room. If you winced, same reason.

Diversity gets the same treatment. Posters in the break room, hashtags in the annual report, training modules that inspire more eyerolls than change. **Representation without redistribution. Inclusion without influence. Celebration without compensation.**

People know immediately when they're decoration instead of decision-makers. They sense when "bring your whole self" means "bring the parts of yourself we find comfortable."

That's not diversity. No one feels included, and equity hasn't been seen in years. It kills the commitment of people whose perspectives could transform how work gets done.

What It's Costing You Personally

This isn't abstract organizational theory. This is your Tuesday morning, your weekend that disappeared into "quick updates," your drive home when you're too exhausted to think but too wired to rest.

The cost shows up in specifics. It sounds like a calendar invite that could have been a Post-it. It looks like a dashboard full of yellow warnings nobody clicks because clicking means owning. It feels like finishing a twelve-hour day and thinking, **"This is not what I'm here for!"**

Here's what happens to high performers specifically: The ones who used to see three moves ahead start waiting for permission. The people who could read a room and shift strategy mid-meeting now rehearse safe talking points. The leaders who built their careers on instinct spend weekends building decks to justify decisions they already know are right.

Your best people can do the work. They're leaving because the work won't let them use what makes them excellent. The pattern recognition that spots problems early gets dismissed as "jumping ahead." The directness that could save three meetings gets labeled "not a team player." The creative solutions get buried under, "That's not how we do things here."

So, they stop offering. They learn the real skill isn't problem-solving. It's looking like you're solving problems while keeping everyone comfortable.

They second-guess instincts that could guide teams through uncertainty. They apologize for expertise that could solve problems. They edit themselves down to safe, unremarkable versions.

The feral confidence that says, "I know how to handle this" gets replaced with "Let me check with my manager."

Exhaustion becomes currency. You earn credibility through late-night emails. You get applause for "going the extra mile," never for asking why the extra mile is always required. The performance review calls you "dedicated" and never asks why dedication looks like depletion instead of craft.

Then comes the cost of translation. The hour you spend rewriting an email, so your truth doesn't scare the system. The meeting where someone asks a real question and the room goes cold. The one-on-one where you say "good" when the truer answer is, "*I spend all day being careful, and that's killing my best thinking.*"

That edit you make to yourself? That's the genuine cost. And it's **compounding interest on a loan you never agreed to take.**

The Systemic Breakdown

So why now? Why does this matter more today than five years ago?

The numbers are brutal. Two-thirds of the workforce is disengaged1. Less than one in three people trust their manager2. That's not a dip. That's a demolition project. And you're somewhere in that story, either not trusting or not being trusted. It might be, you're both.

But this isn't about statistics. It's about what happens when the smartest people in organizations learn that silence is safer than solutions. When the ones who can read three moves ahead start editing themselves into nothing. When feral intelligence gets buried so deep that people forget they ever had it.

Here's what that looks like on a Thursday morning.

Nonprofit staff huddle. Folding chairs, donated table, coffee cooling faster than the energy in the room.

The executive director carries both the mission and the terror of losing the funders who keep the lights on. The agenda says, "strategic priorities." The conversation circles grant reporting templates. Deadlines. Metrics. *Deliverables* and *optics* barge in like uninvited relatives.

Staff shift in their seats. Everyone knows the community they serve needs a different approach. One the current plan doesn't cover. One that would work.

Nobody says it.

The director, trying to demonstrate accountability to people who will never see this room, doubles down on the reporting form. The funder's deadline drowns out the community's need. When the meeting ends, staff leave with calendars packed, spreadsheets full, and the quiet grief of watching the real work slip through their fingers again.

No villains in the room. Only good intentions strangled by bad systems.

The people in that room know exactly how to serve their community. They have the expertise, the relationships, the instincts to navigate complexity. But they've learned that speaking up costs more than staying quiet and they stop offering what they know.

Organizations pay the price in fragility. The surface gleams while the interior rots. When pressure hits, and pressure always hits, systems crack exactly where trust should have been load-bearing.

Strategy thins because strategic thinking requires naming uncomfortable truths out loud. Innovation dies because genuine innovation demands confidence that you can recover from mistakes, not permission to avoid them.

Trust becomes performance. "I trust you" followed by requests for hourly updates. Leaders say "empowerment" but signal surveillance. Teams offer care that lands as criticism.

When the breakdown becomes complete, collaboration becomes compliance. Meetings turn into recitals where everyone performs competence, and nobody risks truth. Decisions float upward because risk isn't allowed to live where the work happens.

The people closest to problems stop naming them. The people furthest from reality make all the calls.

This is how brilliant organizations become brittle. This is how cultures that once moved fast learn to move carefully. **This is the cost of domestication at scale.**

The Great Forgetting

This leads to the most dangerous cost: **cultures forget.**

People forget what it felt like to be fully awake at work. They forget the rush of a wild idea landing in the right room at the right moment. They forget what their voice sounded like before they learned to soften it. They forget their own competence because the system keeps rewarding performance over practice, compliance over contribution.

Watch it happen in real time. Someone walks into a meeting with an idea so alive it lights up their face. They open their mouth. They see the room. They tuck it away. After enough rounds of that, they stop bringing ideas altogether. The chairs stay full. The room goes hollow.

The Great Forgetting doesn't announce itself. It accumulates. One swallowed idea. One edited truth. One moment of choosing safety over signal. It compounds until people can't remember what they sounded like before they learned to translate everything into language the system could tolerate.

Senior leaders forget they ever questioned authority. Mid-level managers forget they once moved fast without asking permission. Individual contributors forget they used to solve problems instead of escalating them. Everyone forgets that work used to feel like creating something instead of surviving something.

Forgetting makes people easy to manage and impossible to guide. Once it sets in, you can't fix it with a new framework or a revised org chart. People don't need better practices. **They need to remember who they were before the system taught them to be smaller.**

They need leadership that doesn't point toward a destination but calls back the intelligence, humor, and nerve they buried to survive. They need someone who sees the feral capacity still flickering underneath the performance and says, "That. Bring that."

The part that knows "I can figure this out" gets buried so deep some people forget it ever existed. But it's still there. Dormant, not dead. Waiting for the right conditions to wake back up.

That's what we're here to do. Not build something new. **Remember what never should have been forgotten.**

The Rebellion Has Already Started

Yet here's the hope: **every system remembers how to be wild.**

Anyone who's ever battled trumpet vine or wisteria knows wildness refuses containment. Clear the field. Spray it down. Pave it over. Give it time, and green shoots crack through concrete. Vines climb fences they were never supposed to touch. Trees muscle up through asphalt. The living will not stay tamed.

Cultures don't shift because someone writes a manifesto. They shift because people like you get tired of the performance. Because the old script stops making sense. Because silence starts costing more than risk.

The tiny rebellions matter too. The Slack message: "Can we please do the work instead of talking about doing the work?" The sticky notes on monitors that say, *Outcomes Only* like a private manifesto. The leader who turns a status meeting into a decision and pretends it was always supposed to work that way.

This opens the door for the team that stops worrying about judgment long enough to ship something that matters. The leader who asks, "What if we just decided?" and everyone realizes no one was stopping them except the mythology that someone else had to approve it first.

These moments are fragile. But they're proof the ground is moving. Proof that underneath all the rituals, people still know how to guide.

Humor has always been the weapon of the feral. It's how sanity gets smuggled back into rooms built for obedience. A whispered joke during a two-hour compliance briefing isn't coping. It's resistance. It keeps alive the part of us that knows this isn't the only way work can happen.

The rebellion isn't coming. **It's already here.** In every person who stops translating their ideas into corporate-speak. In every team that prioritizes the problem over the process. In every leader who trusts their people enough to let them figure it out instead of performing certainty they don't have.

You're not alone in this. You never were.

Guides and Guards: A Choice for Change

Guides are not mythical. You've met them.

They're often the very people the system tried to push out. Branded too difficult. Too intense. Too opinionated. Too sensitive. Too blunt. Too curious. Sometimes it's perspective, sometimes experience, sometimes neurodivergent wiring. The point is: **difference isn't a footnote. It's what makes a guide.**

Think back to the manager who didn't just cover for you when you messed up, but walked into the room beside you, shoulder to shoulder, making sure the mistake didn't erase your worth. The colleague who caught your half-formed idea, gave it space, and asked the question that made it stronger.

These are guides. They don't need the title. You know them because something in you steadies when they're in the room. **That's the gift: safety and courage in the same breath.** The relief of not burning energy on self-protection. The permission to risk more, create more, speak more because someone else is holding ground with you.

Then there's the other stance. **Guardship.** Well-meaning, often earnest, born from genuine care. The leader who hides behind policy to keep everyone safe. The exec who mistakes oversight for protection. The manager who says "I'm just trying to make sure nothing goes wrong" while slowly suffocating every innovative idea under layers of approval.

Guards aren't villains. They believe they're protecting people. And sometimes, in genuinely dangerous situations, protection matters. But **guardship in the wrong context becomes a cage.** It extracts safety instead of generating it. It trades possibility for control. And over time, it teaches people that the way to stay safe is to stay small.

All guides are leaders, but not all leaders are guides. When we confuse the two, when we promote guards into roles that require guides, cultures thin out. Trust erodes. Hope shrinks. Innovation dies waiting for permission that will never feel safe enough to give.

Ecology has language for this. **Monoculture**: rows of identical crops, easy to manage, efficient to harvest, one storm away from total collapse. **Ecosystem:** messy, layered, interdependent, resilient, alive. Guides embody biodiversity. They're roots at different depths, canopy that shares light, mycelia underfoot carrying nourishment where it's needed most.

Guardship can be redirected. It takes intention, reflection, and the courage to ask: Am I protecting people or controlling outcomes? Am I creating safety or demanding certainty?

The difference matters. One builds capacity. The other buries it.

This Moment Belongs to Us

The landscape has always been uneven. But right now, pressure is rising in every direction: political chaos, ecological reckoning, economic volatility, technological disruption that makes last quarter's strategy look like a cave painting. Fragile systems will shatter. Resilient ones will bend, adapt, and keep moving.

And the beautiful part: **everything organizations need to survive and thrive, you carry**.

That pattern recognition they called "jumping ahead"? That's the early warning system they're about to desperately need. The systems thinking they dismissed as "overcomplicating things"? That's the only lens that works when complexity stops pretending to be simple. Your ability to sense what's coming before the dashboard lights up? That's worth more than every consultant deck in the building. Your willingness to name what everyone else is carefully not mentioning? That's the difference between adapting and collapsing.

The organizations that make it won't be the ones with the smoothest performance rituals or the most polished leadership brand. They'll be the ones with actual roots: trust deep enough to hold during storms, competence distributed across the entire system instead of hoarded at the top, expertise trusted to surface solutions instead of buried under process.

The choice is simple. Keep performing certainty while the world shifts underneath or **start guiding through the uncertainty with clarity and nerve**. Keep rehearsing control while trust erodes or **build a culture where people don't need permission** to solve problems. Whether they remember that leadership isn't about having all the answers, but **having the confidence you can find them.**

This moment belongs to guides. The ones who ask questions that make rooms uncomfortable and decisions better. The ones who've been called "too much" their whole lives and are now realizing that "too much" is exactly the voltage this moment requires.

That's you. You know it is. And what comes next? That's where it gets interesting.

We Are Changing How Leadership Works

If you've been nodding, laughing, cringing a little, you already know **you're not broken. The exhaustion isn't weakness. It's proof you're awake in a system designed to keep people sedated.**

The discomfort you feel? That's not inadequacy. That's your feral intelligence recognizing it was built for something more alive than this endless performance.

You're still in there. The part that reads what's happening in meetings while everyone else recites their talking points. The instinct that knows what will work versus what will photograph well for the board. The ability to solve problems and navigate chaos even when the system fights you at every turn.

Here's the thing: **you don't need to become something new. You need to remember what you are.** Someone with the competence, instincts, and nerve to guide others through ground that won't stop shifting. Someone who doesn't need permission to see clearly, name what's true, or trust your own read on what matters.

We're changing how leadership works. Not by stacking another framework on the mountain of frameworks gathering dust. Not by teaching people to fake confidence they don't feel. **We're remembering what was always true:** the intelligence, courage, and creativity organizations desperately need lives in the people who've been told to tone it down.

You don't need permission to tell the truth about what's broken. And you don't need a perfect plan before you start. You need the guts to take one step and trust you'll figure out the next one.

> Truth isn't insubordination. Truth is the only foundation that can hold weight.

The method is simple. Three elements: **Seeds of Potential** (the living capacities already in you), **Guideship** (the stance that lets you lead, follow, or manage as each moment demands), and **Signal** (how your intention moves through culture and becomes impact people experience).

But here's what matters most: **you're not learning from scratch. You're reclaiming what got buried.** What comes next isn't about becoming someone else. It's about coming home to who you've been all along, before the system taught you to make yourself smaller.

The world doesn't need more polished leaders performing wisdom they don't have. It needs guides who trust their instincts, recover from mistakes without collapsing, and create space for others to bring their full focus without apology. Organizations that can bend without shattering because they're built on human capacity, not compliance rituals.

That's not a vision. **That's the work.** And it starts the moment people like you decide "too much" was never the problem.

It was always the exact right dose.

Ready?

[1] Gallup, *What Followers Want*, 2023. [2] DDI, *Global Leadership Forecast 2025*.

SIGNAL CHECK

SELF

What intelligence have you been translating into "corporate" before you speak, and what would you sound like if you trusted that your untranslated truth is what's actually needed?

TEAM

When we think about The Great Forgetting, the moments we've learned to tuck ideas away instead of speaking them, what conditions would help us remember what we knew before we learned to be smaller?

CULTURE

Looking at the organization right now, are we rewarding Guides (people who create safety and courage in the same breath) or Guards (people who mistake oversight for protection), and what shifts if we redistribute influence accordingly?

Two

The Compass for The Curious

The Method · Ecosystemic Leadership

Leadership happens at the edges.

Not in the corner office or the boardroom or the retreat center with its flip charts and motivational posters. Leadership happens where two systems meet. Where departments bump into each other. Where strategy collides with reality. Where your team's expertise meets a customer's problem.

In ecology, these places have a name: **ecotones**. The boundary zones where forest meets grassland, river meets floodplain, ocean meets shore. These edges aren't chaotic messes. They're the most alive places in any system. More species, more activity, more creative collisions. More signal.

The same is true in organizations. The edges hum with possibility, but many people flee to the safety of the interior where everything is predictable, manageable, controlled. They miss the vitality. They miss where the real work gets done.

Guides lean toward the edge. They know that's where understanding and exploration lives, where problems get solved, where cultures shift. They don't tolerate the messiness of boundaries. They thrive there.

The Curiosetti Method™ was built for the edges. Not another framework to memorize, but a living system that helps you navigate the spaces where certainty evaporates, and maps become useless. Where you need something more than a checklist.

You need a compass.

Why We Crumble Near the Edge

The problem with pyramids, matrices, and step-by-step processes: they assume leadership happens in straight lines. Do A, get B. Follow the framework, achieve success. Check the boxes, earn the promotion.

Real leadership doesn't work that way. Real leadership is jazz, not classical music. It's improvisation, adaptation, reading the room and responding to what's alive right now. It's knowing when to lead, when to manage, when to follow, and how to shift between them without losing your footing.

Most models flatten people into compliance. They reward the predictable, measure what looks tidy on a dashboard, and systematically train the edges out of leaders. They want innovation from people they've taught not to innovate. They demand agility from cultures built on approval layers.

That's not leadership development. **That's domestication.**

The Curiosetti Method™ takes a different approach. Instead of trying to tame your edges, it helps you use them with intention. Instead of flattening you into someone else's idea of leadership, it builds on what's feral, original, and alive in you.

Three elements working together like a compass in uncertain terrain: **Seeds of Potential**, **Guideship**, and **Signal**. Not skills to acquire, but capacities to cultivate. Not positions to hold, but stances to embody. Not messages to broadcast, but presence to align.

The Lie About the I

You know the line. *"There's no I in team."*

Every office has a poster with it somewhere. You've had it tossed at you when someone wants to shut down a disagreement. Everyone rolls their eyes because they know exactly what it means: sit down, shut up, stop being difficult.

That phrase is corporate nonsense. And funny how it's always said by the person whose "I" already takes up all the space in the room.

Teams are nothing but individuals. Identities. Ideas. Instincts. Irritations. All those forces colliding are what make the work alive. Pretending otherwise doesn't build unity. It builds compliance. That's not a team. That's a performance troupe where everyone pretends to agree, then escapes to the hallway to whisper what they think.

You've lived this. The meeting where someone shares a raw idea, half-formed, not slide-ready, and you watch it die on the table. The leader says, "Interesting," but their face says, *Not today*. Everyone else leans back, relieved it wasn't their idea gasping for air. The oxygen leaves the room.

That's what "no I in team" looks like in practice.

Now picture the opposite. The moment one person's individuality saved the day. The new hire who spotted the risk no one else saw. The assistant who said, "This process is broken," and fixed it. The manager who said, "Stop, this isn't safe," and prevented harm.

Those weren't consensus moments. They were individual sparks refusing to disappear.

My act of cheeky recognition of every unrecognized effort? I built this entire framework on "I" words to break that cliché forever. Sometimes rebellion starts with a laugh.

Every time you hear "there's no I in team," grin like you've got a secret and think, *There are eight, actually. And they're busy rewriting the rules while you're quoting posters.*

Because the joke's on them. A team without individuals isn't a team. It's a cult of sameness. Real teams are ecosystems, not monocultures. The canopy is uneven, the roots tangle at different depths, and the understory fills every gap. Teams survive because difference keeps the complete system breathing.

When someone pulls that tired line, don't swallow it. Laugh a little. Maybe even out loud.

Then remember: every capacity you carry holds power. The work of leadership is expansion and amplification.

That's where we begin. With individuals refusing to shrink, and leaders who finally know how to grow them.

The Seeds of Potential: Your Living Capacities

I love the moss in the mountains and its steadfast reclamation of wood and stone. Creating life, wrapping its green lushness over the roughest terrain, patient as a glacier and twice as determined. It will thrive anywhere given a chance. In the dead of winter, I can brush back leaves and find brilliant green moss carrying on, thriving. Watching that slow-motion geological feast rearranged my brain.

That's what potential looks like when it's unleashed. Not polite. Not manageable. **Alive**.

The Seeds of Potential aren't personality traits you either have or don't. They're not boxes to check off some competency grid designed by people who've never led through chaos. They're living capacities that thrive with attention or drift without it.

Think biodiversity. In healthy ecosystems, variety builds resilience. Monocultures look efficient until they collapse spectacularly. Leadership works the same way. A team strong in innovation but weak in integration creates brilliant ideas that die in committee. A culture that values independence but neglects inclusion burns out its strongest contributors while congratulating itself on "high performance."

Seven Seeds, plus the soil that feeds them all. They don't sprout politely one at a time. They tangle together like roots, creating the complex, adaptive intelligence you need to thrive at the edges.

Inquisitive. Your capacity for collective curiosity that cuts through nonsense to reveal what's real. You don't just ask questions; you pursue understanding that drives progress. Critical thinking. Systems thinking. Creative problem-solving. You ask uncomfortable questions three meetings before the crisis hits. You're not difficult. You're useful.

This is pattern recognition in action. Walking into a room and immediately sensing who's struggling, even when they're smiling. Reading team tension three meetings before it explodes. Seeing connections others miss because you're willing to look where others won't.

Intention. Your capacity to align decisions with purpose instead of politics. You focus energy on what matters most and resist the noise that scatters momentum. Strategic thinking. Prioritization. Accountability. This happens when you stop apologizing for seeing what others miss and start speaking power instead of professionalism.

Intention is your compass. Not just "having goals," but holding the why steady when the how gets messy. Deciding what you're *for* and letting that steer what you're willing to fight for, cut, or protect. It's what keeps you oriented when everyone else is spinning.

Independence. Your capacity to act with agency instead of waiting for permission from people who wouldn't recognize good judgment if it introduced itself with a fancy business card and a sizzle reel. Self-leadership. Decision-making. Courage. Not lone-wolf heroics, but empowerment that moves work forward while others schedule meetings about meetings.

This is the capacity to hold your stance when the room tilts. To calmly say, "We're not doing that," when everyone else is nodding along to a bad idea. Independence keeps you from dissolving into groupthink, but it also keeps you from collapsing into cowardice.

Improvisational. Your capacity to treat disruption as raw material instead of an existential threat. When everything's on fire, who does everyone turn to? Not the person with the prettiest org chart. You. The one who can navigate uncertainty with clarity.

This is adaptability in motion. Not frantic thrashing, but the jazz of leadership: taking what's in front of you and shaping it into something new. What happens when the plan breaks, and instead of panic, you find rhythm.

Inventive. Your capacity to build what doesn't exist instead of perfecting what's broken. Innovation. Creative risk-taking. Visioning. You challenge norms that protect comfort over progress. You imagine possibilities and move from idea to execution without getting trapped in approval circles.

The spark. The refusal to settle for "best practice" when you know the situation demands something different. How you carve new paths when the old ones collapse. How you stop recycling answers that failed.

Integration. Your capacity to connect pieces others keep in separate silos. Systems thinking. Collaboration. Alignment. You bring strategy and execution together. People and processes. Vision and reality. You do it without losing your mind in translation.

This might be the hardest one. It's alignment inside and outside, values and actions, words, and impact. Where authenticity lives, but also where hypocrisy gets exposed. When you integrate, people stop watching your mouth and start trusting your stance.

Intuition. Your capacity to sense patterns before the data catches up. Emotional intelligence. Empathy. Relational judgment. That "too early" timing that makes linear thinkers uncomfortable? That's your competitive advantage. You read what others miss and act with wisdom that includes but transcends analysis.

We've been taught to distrust it, but intuition is a leadership instrument. It's what keeps you from walking your team into the fire when the numbers say everything is fine.

Inclusion. The eighth Seed that runs through all seven like mycelium connecting a forest floor. Belonging. Equity. Psychological safety. Not a side project. It's the connective tissue that lets every other capacity reach its potential.

Without Inclusion, innovation serves the same three voices. Independence tips into arrogance. Intention becomes control. Inclusion is what creates the connection between capacities, amplifying, and growing an ecosystem vs. silos.

It's easy to overlook that they don't show up alone. Each shows up as a constellation of competencies and brings friends along. They'll show up and amplify each other in tension, in rhythm with each other. A crisis might call upon Improvisational, Intention, and Independence at once. Strategy might demand Integration, Intuition, and Inquisitive working together.

Consider them a distillation of the many competencies into the very important competencies for the future.

Guideship: Leadership That Lives at the Edges

A lot of what we call leadership feels more like a performance than a genuine guiding force. Think of those elaborate costumes, scripted lines, and carefully choreographed interactions that seem impressive from afar. But if you peek behind the curtain, you'll see the whole thing unravel.

Now, let's talk about Guideship. It's about being present, not putting on a show. It's about earning respect, not demanding it. It's about finding clarity in the chaos, creating safety in the unknown, and inspiring action when everyone else is stuck in place.

Guideship is the leadership we're all hungry for, that "big L" Leadership w're chasing, not the "little l" leadership that's bossing people around with small energy and even smaller impact.

Let's talk about raft guides.

The first time you have a chance to watch a raft guide work, it's disorienting. Ten strangers clutching paddles like weapons, trying not to look terrified. No time for icebreakers or team-building exercises. The river doesn't wait.

In five minutes, they've done what some people can't do in five months: create enough cohesion, trust, and focus to keep everyone moving in the same direction through whitewater.

How? By understanding a nuance people miss:

Guideship isn't a fixed position. It's adaptive movement.

First, they follow. Not the river yet, but the people. They notice who's cracking nervous jokes, who's white-knuckling their paddle, and who's scanning for exits. Following means observing. Listening without rushing. Watching body language. Hearing the unsaid. You can't guide what you haven't noticed.

Then, they manage. Structure without suffocation. They assign seats, organize equipment, and teach rhythm.

No rhythm, no trust. No coordination, no progress. Managing isn't always glamorous, but it's what allows everyone else to move in sync. Structure frees energy for what matters.

Only then do they lead. They call everyone in, set the tone, and give instructions with clarity that cuts through panic. Leadership here is earned, not assumed. It comes from stance and presence built through observation and coordination.

When the boat hits the rapids, leadership becomes directive and accountable. "Forward two strokes!" "Right Side!" Correction happens in real time. There's no private performance review when the rapid is thirty yards away.

That's Guideship. The art of shifting between stances as the terrain demands. Sometimes you lead, sometimes you manage, sometimes you follow. The sequence matters, as does the reading of the moment. And they did it in board shorts and Chacos.

Leadership programs often miss this. They treat it like a job description, an equation, not a living breathing system. They assume you should always be "leading" instead of realizing that sometimes the most powerful move is to step back, coordinate, or listen.

Guides know something the performance artists don't. **You can't do it alone**. Everyone in the raft has agency. If they don't paddle when you call, the boat slams into a rock. If they over-paddle because they're showing off, you lose balance. The mission only works when everyone owns their part.

Guideship is a choice, not a title. A title gives authority. It doesn't guarantee followership. Presence makes you a guide. Orientation makes you a guide. Because it's a choice, it catches on fast. People feel it, trust it, and start doing it too.

Guides create more guides, not through command but by building enough trust and clarity that others step into their own stance willingly.

One of my favorite quotes comes from an old horseman, a legend in modern relationship-based horse-training, Ray Hunt. He said, "First you go with them, then they go with you, then you go together." And if that doesn't sum up a Guide in action, nothing else will.

Recovery: The Guide's Secret Weapon

What separates real guides from the ones who only look the part is simple. **Guides build recovery into success itself.**

Drift happens. You meant to build trust, but your follow-up felt like control. You intended to empower but your questions landed like interrogation. You aimed for inclusion, but your decision reinforced the same old voices. Drift meant well, but landed wrong.

Traditional leadership calls this failure. The performers burn energy trying to appear flawless, hiding mistakes, spinning every stumble into a learning moment.

Guides know better.

> **Drift, with repair, builds deeper trust than perfection ever can.**

The real magic here is in timely ownership, feedback, and a directional change. It's all about spotting when your message takes a little detour from what you meant to say and then smoothly steering things back on track. This way, you can save everyone from the emotional rollercoaster that would come with trying to fix things yourself!

I realize what I said landed differently than I meant. Let me try again.

I can see this conversation isn't going where either of us wanted. Can we reset?

I was so focused on the deadline that I steamrolled your input. That's not how I want to work with you.

Signal strength looks like this. It shows you're paying attention. You care more about the relationship than your image, and you're capable of course-correcting without losing your footing.

Obstruction is different. That's the choice to abandon Guideship entirely. Avoiding clarity. Disengaging when presence is required. Lack of agency, lack of accountability. Obstruction can take hold, like poison ivy, and it can make people feel like they need to hide or stop talking altogether.

The difference between Drift and Obstruction? Intent and recovery. Drift acknowledged and repaired builds resilience. Obstruction without accountability corrodes trust.

Signal: How Intention Becomes Impact

Think about a time you meant well and it went sideways. You thought you were coaching; they thought you were criticizing. You thought you were being helpful; they heard control. Your intention was good. The impact wasn't.

That's Signal. Not what you mean to communicate, but what others perceive, receive, and believe.

Signal moves in three stages, and each one matters:

Perceive happens the instant someone sees you. Tone. Posture. Expression. Before you say a word, people are scanning and drawing conclusions.

Receive is the exchange. Words, rhythm, the weight in your voice. This is where good intentions can misfire. Words. Rhythm. Weight. You think you're being clear; they hear pressure. You think you're being encouraging; they hear critique.

Believe is what lingers. People don't remember what you said, they remember what they think you meant. If they believe you're steady and fair, they give you grace. If they believe you're self-serving, every slip confirms it.

Most leaders obsess over the first stage. They polish decks, rehearse lines, perform confidence. But Signal isn't a show. It's consistency over time.

And it's not only about others. It's about you. You carry your own internal network of perception, reception, and belief. The critic that turns feedback into failure. The story that tells you you're not enough. The echo of every message that still shapes your confidence.

That's why impostor syndrome sinks its claws so deep. Others misread your Signal. Then you took their confusion as evidence and told yourself you were broken.

Signal in Practice

This understanding of Signal moves through organizations, the way nutrients move through soil. Sometimes nourishing, sometimes creating imbalance, sometimes building up in ways that become toxic over time. In healthy ecosystems, information flows freely.

In unhealthy systems, communication breaks down. Information gets hoarded, filtered, or distorted. Parts of the system become isolated, making decisions based on incomplete or outdated information. The system becomes brittle, vulnerable to collapse when pressure hits.

Guides understand that **healthy Signal is the foundation of healthy systems.** They work to align what they intend with what people perceive, receive, and believe. Not by controlling the message, but by attending to their presence.

They know that Signal operates at every level. One-to-one trust. One-to-team rhythm. System-wide patterns that decide whether intelligence circulates or stagnates.

Signal travels faster than strategy. It spreads wider than policy. It shapes culture more than any speech.

A leader who says "I trust you" followed by requests for hourly updates creates Signal confusion. The words say trust; the behavior screams control. People believe the behavior.

A culture that celebrates innovation in all-hands meetings while punishing failure in performance reviews creates Signal dissonance. People stop believing the praise.

Signal alignment isn't perfection. It's steady integrity between intention and impact. It's noticing when your Signal missed and changing behavior, not spinning explanation.

Guides pay attention to edges because that's where Signal begins. Customer complaints that haven't reached the C-suite yet. Burnout that hasn't hit survey data yet. Ideas that don't fit the old categories yet.

They build relationships with edge-dwellers. The rep. The manager. The bridge-builder who sees trouble or opportunity first. They open pathways that let signals move. Real conversations beyond status updates. Skip-level talks without filters. Networks that keep intelligence alive.

In a changing world, early Signal detection isn't just smart. It's survival.

Where Feral Meets Functional

Seeds give you capacity. Guideship is your stance. Signal shows your impact.

Here's how it looks in real time.

You're leading through change.

Intuition picks up anxiety before it's spoken. **Inquisitive** asks questions that surface what's real. **Integration** connects human impact to results. **Intention** keeps you focused on what matters most when everything feels unstable. Your *Guideship* stance shifts. Observe before acting. Coordinate before directing. Lead when clarity is needed. Your *Signal* stays honest, grounded, hopeful.

You're influencing up in a risk-averse culture.

Independence gives you courage to speak truth. **Inclusion** helps you find language that lands. **Improvisational** thinking lets you adapt in real time. **Inventive** capacity opens new paths when approval layers block progress. Your *Guideship* follows first to read the terrain, then leads with credibility. Your *Signal* builds trust through consistent action.

You're navigating a crisis with half the data.

Improvisation helps you move anyway. **Inquisitive** demands better input. **Integration** balances competing priorities. **Intention** holds your compass steady while uncertainty swirls. Your Guideship gets directive. Clarity and speed matter more than consensus. Your Signal admits what you don't know while projecting confidence you'll find the way.

The method adapts because **you** adapt. The Seeds grow stronger with practice. Your Guideship becomes more fluid as you learn to read terrain. Your Signal sharpens as you stay aligned between intention and impact.

This is regenerative leadership. Leadership that strengthens the system instead of draining it. Leadership that builds capacity instead of dependency. Leadership that spreads wisdom instead of control.

What's Happening Now

The ground is shifting under our feet economically, politically, technologically, culturally. The leaders who keep trying to control their way through uncertainty will exhaust themselves and everyone around them.

The future belongs to guides. People who see patterns others miss. People who ask the challenging questions. People who create space for intelligence to emerge. Not because they know everything, but because they can navigate edges where answers don't exist yet.

Everything organizations need. Innovation. Adaptability. Resilience. Trust. It all happens at the edges. In the collision zones where perspectives meet and the future takes shape.

But for guides, that's home. The place where your feral nature comes alive. Where your ability to read *Signal* and respond creatively becomes the advantage. Where your willingness to lean into uncertainty becomes strength for everyone around you.

The Method shifts your perspective. **It starts with trusting what you know, building on what's alive in you, and bringing your full intelligence to the edges where leadership happens.**

Hey, no need to ask for permission! Just remember that the "too much" you've always been isn't the issue.

It's the solution.

You were never built for obedience or burnout. You were built for movement, imagination, and impact. This is the work that brings you back to life.

The edges are waiting.

SIGNAL CHECK

SELF

Which of the Seeds of Potential do you reach for most naturally under pressure, and which one, if you strengthened it, would transform how you navigate the edges where your best work happens?

TEAM

When we think about the edges where our work comes alive, where systems collide and uncertainty lives, what does Guideship look like for us at our best, and how do we recognize when it's time to shift our stance?

CULTURE

Where in the organization are people already thriving at the edges, reading Signal early and adapting with clarity, and what would amplify their influence across the system?

CHAPTER TWO: THE COMPASS FOR THE CURIOUS

Three

The Audacity of Identity

Experience · Originality · Presence

What's your leadership style?

Why does that question feel like a trap? You already know the face you'll make. The voice you'll use. Just enough edge to sound real, not enough to get flagged. Your shoulders tense. Your mouth edits. You replay the voicemail, reread the email, scan the text. Not for clarity. For tone. For how easily it could be used against you.

Yeah. We're going there.

This chapter is about remembering who you were before they convinced you that your edges needed filing down. Before they taught you that your natural way of seeing was somehow *wrong*. Before you learned to apologize for being brilliant.

Impostor syndrome can die right here. Bring your whole self to the leadership challenges that truly matter.

Your Feral Intelligence

Every room where decisions get made has the same energy. Boardrooms, yes, but also school committee meetings, nonprofit strategy sessions, community planning gatherings. You walk in, and something shifts in your chest. Not anxiety, exactly. More like your entire system recognizing: *This place wasn't built for people like me.*

But while they were trying to tame you, they missed something. **Your experience made you.**

Those late nights troubleshooting problems nobody else could solve. The project that failed spectacularly and taught you more than any success. The client who trusted you with their crisis. The team member who quit because of something you did wrong, and how that changed how you listen. The promotion you earned. The recognition you didn't get. The risks you took. The mistakes you owned.

This is your feral intelligence.
And someone, somewhere along the way, convinced you it was a problem.

All of it lives in your body now as intelligence. Pattern recognition so rapid it feels like intuition yet carries the weight of everything you've witnessed, endured, survived, and learned. This wisdom carries memory. The cultural codes that kept your people alive. The neighborhood that taught you how to read a room. The family dynamics that showed you power works differently than the textbooks claim.

You've been told your curiosity is "too much." Your questions come "too early." Your insights arrive before anyone's ready to hear them. You've learned to fold your edges inward, so no one gets cut on your truth.

But recognize this: this method grows around you. Around your strengths, your cultural identity, your challenges, your victories. All of it. You conform to nothing. The approach meets you where you are, wild edges intact.

Your experience database holds what you lived through and figured out, the real training ground. The time you kept a team together during the merger when leadership vanished. The crisis you navigated by trusting your gut when the data said everything was fine. The relationship you rebuilt after breaking trust. The time you stood alone because standing together wasn't an option.

Every moment of your life has been depositing wisdom into your nervous system. Every success, every failure, every time you chose courage over comfort, every time you didn't. That's not just background noise. That's your competitive advantage.

The Artificial Divide

Institutional power has created the most absurd division between how we're *supposed* to lead and how real change happens.

Expectations

Follow the process. Stay in your lane. Wait for permission. Speak only when spoken to. Innovation through approved channels only, please.

Reality

Hallway conversations. Kitchen table negotiations. Someone finally asking the question everyone's thinking. Moving with authentic presence instead of rehearsed gestures.

This divide didn't happen by accident. It emerged from the endless pursuit of scalability, replicability, and risk management. Systems wanted leadership they could standardize, package, and sell. Something they could teach in modules, measure in assessments, and control through performance reviews.

Most importantly? Something that would preserve existing power structures without challenging anyone's comfortable assumptions about who gets to lead and how.

They built leadership like they build hamburgers: same ingredients, same process, same predictable result. No surprises. No mess. No wild ideas and associative thoughts disrupting the quarterly projections.

What they built was sanitized leadership. Innovation locked behind approved processes, feedback flowing only through sanctioned channels, challenge happening only in designated sessions, like we've scheduled honesty for Tuesdays from 2-3 PM.

We keep saying innovation is absent from our organizations because we've made it impossible to access what's breathing under all that bureaucracy.

Real work happens when someone drops the script and tells the truth. When the budget meeting turns into strategy because someone had the audacity to connect two ideas that weren't supposed to touch. Real transformation emerges when you stop rehearsing and start moving with authentic presence.

Buried Intelligence

Most of us have been trained out of our edges since we could barely tie our shoes.

Remember elementary school? Raise your hand. Wait your turn. Speak only when called on. This wasn't education. This was boot-camp for corporate compliance. Training you to fit into a box so you could one day climb out of it and call it success.

You want to see my kindergarten report card? My mother still has it, naturally. "Linda talks too much. Linda won't stay in her seat. Linda is so smart *if she would only...*"

There it is. The original wound. The first time someone told a feral child that her fire was too bright, her questions too many, her movement too much. The moment they started teaching me that my natural state was *a problem to be solved.*

Ring a bell?

Systems perfected this conditioning. The devil's advocate with deep care for the project gets told to be "more positive." The visionary gets locked into meetings designed for entirely different attention spans. Job descriptions get written in the most common language for the most uncommon humans.

The cruel part? We assault people with development toward some mythological standard while telling them we love what they "bring to the table." Development plans ignore your 95% brilliance to obsess over that 5% gap. You're leading breakthrough projects, building trust across impossible divides, creating solutions no one else sees, but sure, let's spend forty-five minutes discussing how you *need to improve your executive presence.*

By the time the process is complete, they're unrecognizable. Packaged. And we wonder why innovation dies on conference room tables.

Cost of Compliance Culture

The unfortunate outcome when everyone learns to color inside the lines? **Most compliant rise while most insightful suffocate.**

Institutions claim to want innovation while punishing its messengers. Teams achieve surface alignment but lose the creative friction that drives real breakthroughs. We've built cultures obsessed with perfectionism and proof when what we need is creative problem-solving and jazz improvisation.

What you sacrifice at the altar of belonging is the very signal that would keep your organization alive when disruption hits. When everyone's singing the same three-chord power ballad, no one can adapt to jazz. Most systems desperately need that jazz to survive. Some could use a full-on punk rock breakdown.

Think about the last real crisis you faced collectively. Who did everyone turn to? Not the person with the AI presentation. The one who navigated complexity with clarity. The one who sensed patterns others missed. The one who translated chaos into action.

Those moments reveal what we value: pattern recognition, flexibility, innovation born of lived experience.

The irony? We develop the guideship right out of guides by stripping away the very qualities that make them effective when everything's on fire. Then we wonder why our organizations can't adapt when the world shifts.

What's this cost to you, your team, your culture? How long have you been performing certainty when your gut knows better?

When We Abandon Ourselves

What survival looks like in these environments.

Most of us received training in *behavior*, not leadership. We learned to read rooms like our lives depended on it because sometimes it did. Sensing tension and calibrating our presence to make others comfortable, even when uncomfortable truths desperately needed a voice.

We learned to shape-shift across contexts. The decisive leader in one meeting, the collaborative partner in another, the empathetic listener in a third. Not from authenticity but from **survival instinct**.

We gave the right emotions. Enthusiasm for initiatives we knew would fail. Measured concern for crises that terrified us. Neutrality when passion was what the moment demanded.

Your cultural identity? Dial it down. Your neurodivergence? Keep it invisible. Your way of processing information? Better learn to mimic their pace. Your accent, your volume, your way of moving through the world? All of it gets edited for their comfort.

These adaptations weren't character flaws. They were survival strategies. Sophisticated responses to systems that were never designed for your full presence.

A client once told me she felt like she had two selves: the one she showed at work, and the one she carried home. At work she was edited, careful, rounding every edge before it left her mouth. At home she ranted, laughed too loud, argued with her kids over dinner, came alive. She wasn't confused about who she was. She was exhausted from splitting herself in two.

It gets exhausting. You don't just split yourself in two. You fracture into ten different versions. The professional self who speaks their language. The family self who carries your real values. The social self who navigates their networks. The version that manages your parents' expectations. The one that code-switches across cultural boundaries. The careful self in predominantly white spaces. The grateful self when they finally notice your work. The invisible self when they can't handle your presence. The masking.

That's what systems do when they train you to perform instead of belong. They teach you to ration your originality like contraband. To keep your signal dimmed until you're in private. People sense the dissonance between all the selves you edit for different audiences and wonder which one is real. Suddenly, even the curated you isn't trustworthy.

The exhausting part? Most people have no idea you're even doing this work. They think you're *just naturally good at fitting in.*

Some of us pay a particularly brutal tax for acceptance. The Black woman who can never express righteous anger, even when repeatedly dismissed. The disabled leader who must appear *grateful* rather than demand proper accommodation. The queer team member who softens their pronouns, so no one feels "uncomfortable." The first-generation professional performing affluence so nobody questions their background. The neurodivergent leader masking their processing style to appear *normal*. The woman who lowers her voice, so she sounds less *intimidating*.

What makes it more exhausting? Most people have no clue about the level of constant adaptation required just to exist in these spaces.

Early Warning Signals

You know her. You might be her.

She walked into meetings knowing exactly what would happen six months out. Market shifts, consumer behavior, competitive threats. She read patterns like weather forecasters read clouds. But the company wanted innovation without disruption, foresight without inconvenience.

She learned to translate. Conditional language, softened approach. Extra smiles. Too many emojis in an email. Package your warnings as questions. "What if we considered..." instead of "This will fail." Wait for external validation before sharing what she knew. Transform her razor-sharp insights into suggestions that wouldn't scare anyone.

They praised her growth. "Much more collaborative now. Really listening to the team."

Her warnings still came true. They just arrived **too late to pivot**.

That's the cost of constant translation. You lose response time. You miss intervention points. You sacrifice the very advantage that made you valuable.

The cruelest part? These adaptations work. You survive, even advance. But **your core nature is trying to save everyone while theirs is trying to preserve the status quo.**

The Curious: Welcome

There's a name for us, you know. Well, there is now.

This spirit of curiosity refuses to die, no matter how much institutional pressure tries to smother it. We are the canaries the system desperately needs but keeps trying to stuff back into cages. We feel earthquake tremors while everyone else admires the architecture. We smell smoke while others debate quarterly budgets.

Look around your team right now. You know who they are. The one who asks the uncomfortable questions in all-hands meetings. The quiet analyst who somehow predicts which projects will implode. The operations person who can smell dysfunction from three departments away. **These are your people.** *Finally.*

The Curious. Not only curious, but an entire population of pattern-weavers, signal-readers, early-warning systems walking around in human form. Associative thinkers, creative thinkers. *Finally.*

You speak up too early. You notice before there's proof. You bring friction before there's buy-in. And you've been told to wait your turn. Or worse, to stop feeling so much.

The beautiful absurdity? They're asking you to dial down the very reasoning that could save them from their own terrible decisions. Like asking a smoke detector to be quieter during a fire.

What makes you dangerous is your ability to integrate.

You don't just collect data. You spy the patterns that reveal what's happening. You analyze *and* synthesize. You feel truth before you can name it, which terrifies people who need three meetings to decide on font choices.

You exist everywhere. The nurse who senses patient decline before vital signs catch up. The teacher who spots brewing tension in conversation patterns everyone else dismisses. The small business owner connecting market signals competitors treat as coincidence. The project manager who knows which initiatives will collapse before the first status meeting.

Consider this: A program director kept making "intuitive leaps" that frustrated their linear colleagues. They'd connect community signals with demographic trends and land on insights that seemed to come from Mars. "Off topic," the team would sigh. "Distracting."

Six months later, when their "wild" predictions came true exactly as called, the team suddenly discovered they were "visionary." They started calling them "synthesis sessions." Because nothing says visionary quite like relabeling what you used to call *off topic*.

The world is accelerating past the comfort zone of step-by-step thinkers. Different times require different solutions require different perspectives require different minds. The future belongs to pattern weavers, signal readers, and people who can sense what's next before the data confirms it. Your "too early" timing? That's about to become your advantage.

Your moment is here. Finally.

Conscious Reclamation

Most systems claim to value authentic insight while systematically training it out of their leaders. They want the benefits of integrated intelligence without the messiness of letting people *embody* it.

Think about that for a second. They're asking for innovation from people they've trained not to innovate.

This is about conscious reclamation. Archaeological work on your own buried brilliance.

Three movements that'll make your nervous system uncomfortable, but will set you free:

Recognize What You've Buried

Your body knows what your mind keeps explaining away. Feel the tension when certain names appear on the meeting invite? The way your voice gets smaller when you're about to share something brilliant? Your nervous system is a built-in safety net, always keeping an eye out. It's way more reliable than any performance review ever could be. It knows when you're in environments that are meant for someone else's comfort, not for your brilliant ideas to shine!

Start treating those signals like data instead of character flaws.

Honor Your Adaptations

Before you spiral into shame about "people-pleasing," pause. That over-preparation that makes you bring three backup plans? That code-switching that lets you navigate hostile environments?

You're not broken. You're brilliant.

A healthcare leader realized her habit of bringing extra data wasn't insecurity. It was a warrior's armor against having her expertise questioned in ways her male colleagues never experienced. She wasn't neurotic; she was *strategic*.

Honor the understanding that kept you safe before deciding what still serves you.

Choose Your Language

This is where it gets transformational. What if you got to name yourself with confidence? What if "too intense" became "high voltage"? What if "too direct" became "efficient"? What if "too extra" became "fully expressed"? What if "too basic" became "grounded"?

You get to choose the language for your presence. Your gender, your presence in the world, your presentation, all of it. Yours to claim as identity. Ours to honor as witness. The words that describe your way of being in the world. Your identity isn't assigned by systems that never understood you.

It's chosen by you, for you, in service of what you're here to do.

Strategic authenticity means bringing your full self to moments where it creates maximum impact. Not performing niceness for people who wouldn't recognize insight if it showed up with talking points and asked to connect on LinkedIn.

Growing Deep, Reaching High

When we only focus on "fixing" ourselves, we forget a milestone. Identity work digs up what's buried and grows new roots at the same time. Both directions, same moment.

Roots deepening.

Every crisis you've navigated equips your nervous system with the ability to remain composed under pressure. Every failure that didn't lead to your demise enhances your capacity for recovery. Every time you were underestimated and proved them wrong serves as evidence of your competence. The cultural wisdom passed down through your family. The street smarts acquired from your neighborhood. The resilience cultivated in environments that weren't initially designed for you.

This isn't merely your personal history. It's your operating system. It's the reason you can step into chaos and find clarity. It's why you sense potential problems before they escalate. It's why people turn to you when everything is on fire.

Think of the work of the roots in a forest. Growing towards gravity, in the dark and mud and no one sees that growth. Yet, there it is feeding and nourishing the tree and part of a thriving system of success.

Branches reaching.

As your roots deepen, you're also growing toward your potential. You claim language that resonates with your presence, intentionally take up space, speak your insights without editing, trust your timing, and refuse to shrink for their comfort.

We're always impressed by the growth in the sunshine. Brilliant greens, tall trees, and bright blooms are just a glimpse of what's happening. Don't give it all the credit.

You can be too much and not enough, and exactly right in the same moment. You can be too intense for some rooms and not intense enough for others, but you're perfectly calibrated for the work that's yours to do.

Don't let your development focus only on one to the detriment of the other. Either polish your presentation or find your authentic voice. But you need both roots that go deep enough to hold you steady and branches that reach far enough to create the change you're here to make.

Standing Whole

This brings us to the heart of it. Take a breath with me. Feel your own body right now. The place where your shoulders meet your neck. The rhythm of air moving through your chest. The weight of your feet on the ground.

Think back. The first time you were told you were "too much." The classroom where your curiosity got graded down. The job interview where you were warned to "tone it back." The family table where silence was safer than truth.

You learned the cost of standing whole. You also learned the cost of disappearing. And still, you're here. Still carrying that Signal. Still alive to the question: what would happen if I stopped editing myself down?

When you edit yourself to fit monoculture leadership, you don't buy trust. You enter captivity. Systems never thank you for dimming. They only ask for more dimming. You'll dim until you vanish.

But when you stand whole? Even once, even shakily, even with your voice breaking? The ground shifts. People exhale. They risk their unfinished thought because you risked yours first.

They straighten their spine because you kept yours.

That's guideship in its rawest form. Not extracting trust but being trustworthy. **To yourself first. Then to others.**

Your identity works as an ecosystem. What you carry inside interplays with what you show outside and what the world feeds you back in return. Every time you show up aligned, you shape that moment and leave an imprint on the culture. A trace. A pathway. Someone else comes along, and the ground is a little less brittle because you stood there whole.

This is where your grounded sense of identity keeps you steady. **Intention** to say no to drift. **Integration** to hold your inside and outside together. **Inclusion** to widen the circle without erasing anyone's difference. **Independence** to resist selling out your stance for applause. **Improvisation** to move when the map ends. **Intuition** to trust your body briefing. **Invention** to make a new way when the old one fails.

These aren't traits to polish for performance reviews. They're daily practices of being trustworthy to yourself.

And they matter now more than ever. Because the world doesn't need more same-shape leaders rehearsing the same script. The world needs the too much, the too quiet, the too slow, the too fast, the too feeling, the too logical. The ones who need three days to process and the ones who know in three seconds. The ones who can feel the current before the room admits it. The world needs you.

Listen.

You are not *too much*. You are not *not enough*. You are **an only**. The **original**. The **OG**. The first, and extremely limited, edition. Only you. And only you can bring that signal into this moment, right now, in the places that need it most.

All of it lives in your body as experience, memory, intuition. Not just what you learned in school or read in books, but what you lived through and figured out. That's your unique ability we'll never see again. That's what makes you irreplaceable. That's why they need you to stay whole.

The Curious inherit the earth. **And it's about time.**

SIGNAL CHECK

SELF

What do you know that you've been softening, rewording, or holding back to fit the room, and what would happen if you trusted that your raw read on the situation is exactly what's needed?

TEAM

As a team, where do we already see The Curious operating among us, the ones who spot patterns early, connect ideas others miss, or sense what's coming, and how do we amplify that instead of asking them to wait their turn?

CULTURE

What becomes possible when we value leaders who can move through uncertainty without pretending it doesn't exist?

FOUR

The Ethos of Reclamation

AGENCY · PURPOSE · INTEGRITY

Do you remember who you are now? The part under the title, the email tone, the filtered face. A dear friend often says, "Remember who the f*** you are!" and says it with such strength in the moment, that I do, indeed, remember who the f*** I am.

I want the same for you. Good. Now what?

Now comes the part that separates insight from impact: **Are you going to do something about it?**

The thing about recognizing the challenge is that nothing changes if you don't move. It's useless until you stop hiding behind good intentions and start making moves that matter. The world doesn't need another person who *gets it*. The world needs guides who get it and act.

You can know exactly who you are and still spend the next decade explaining why you're not ready to show up as that person yet.

Agency over obligation. Decision over default.

This chapter is about crossing from knowing better to doing better. From endless strategizing to skin-in-the-game leadership that changes rooms, relationships, and results.

Fair warning: This is where most people retreat to the planning phase. It's safer to stay in analysis mode than step onto the field where your choices have consequences and everyone can see whether you mean what you say.

But you're not most people. You're The Curious. And The Curious don't keep themselves hidden when the world needs what you've got.

But before we go there, I need you to get something specific in your head.

What's the one thing you know, but aren't doing, right now?

Mmhmmm, that one. Not a list. One thing. The conversation you keep postponing. The decision you're pretending still needs more information. The dream you're workshopping instead of building. The boundary you know needs to exist, but you keep explaining away.

These crossings don't hold much significance until you apply them to something that evokes a slight sense of fear. Something with consequences. Something where your decision sacrifices your comfort.

It could be the moment you finally express your true thoughts to your boss. You're acknowledging that your marriage requires a different approach than it did five years ago. You're shedding the outdated identity that society expects you to maintain.

Got it? Good. Hold onto that. Now let's talk about what it takes to cross.

The Crossings That Matter

A funny thing about leadership? We've turned it into a collecting hobby. Merit badges, certificates, frameworks to memorize and forget by Thursday. Meanwhile, you're sitting in meetings watching someone with zero self-awareness make decisions that'll torpedo the whole project.

Your reticence to respond when they ask for your "input" when you know they've already decided? That's your nervous system filing its report: **This is playacting, not leadership.**

A lot of leadership development seems designed to keep you small. Compliant. Asking permission. Waiting for someone more qualified to show up and save the day.

There's no glory in *noticing* a threshold.

You either cross, or spend your whole life explaining why you're not ready yet.

- **AGENCY:** The moment you stop asking "Can I?" and start asking "What now?"

- **ACTION:** When your behavior finally matches what you say you believe. No more gap between Sunday values and Monday choices.

- **CAPACITY:** The terror and thrill of realizing you can handle way more than you thought. *You've been doing it all along.*

- **KNOWLEDGE:** Stop treating expertise like a secret you're not allowed to tell. Use what you know.

Let me tell you about *leadership taxidermy.*

I'm trapped in a conference room that feels like a museum for dead ideas. For 90 minutes we categorize leadership styles like we're organizing a spice rack. Democratic here, autocratic there, transformational in the corner collecting dust.

Nobody asks what keeps you staring at the ceiling at 3 AM. Nobody wants to know what choice you've been dodging since your last performance review turned into an *unqualified* therapy session about "areas for growth."

Leadership taxidermy. All the appearance of the beast with none of the wild, beating heart. They're stuffing and mounting concepts that should be alive, breathing, and occasionally snapping us back to reality.

You've been the person nodding along while internally screaming. Thinking if you just collect enough certifications, someday you'll feel qualified to use the brain you were born with.

You're already qualified. The question is whether you're brave enough to act like it.

There are four crossings, and they arrive in order. Each one demands a new decision, and each asks the same question before the door opens: *will you make the decision and move forward?*

Agency: The First Crossing

Choice (noun)

The power to move your own story. Stop waiting to be picked. The instant you decide your purpose matters more than their comfort and act like it.

To Choose (verb)

To claim your freedom to decide and your responsibility for what follows. To move with intention, not permission. To remember that power unused is still a choice. One that keeps you small.

Here's something that might make HR squirm: **Agency is precisely why leadership development should never be mandatory.** Compliance training? Absolutely. Safety protocols? Required. But development? Make it optional and watch what happens.

Saving seats for the unwilling is a leadership habit long past its prime. That person rolling their eyes in the back row, convinced this is beneath them? Believe them. That's your future toxic leader, already poisoning every room they enter. Meanwhile, you're gatekeeping the people who want to grow to accommodate someone who can't be bothered.

When promotion time comes and they're surprised they got passed over, remind them: agency is a choice. And they chose poorly.

Give that opportunity to the person already showing engagement, curiosity, purpose, and trust. Yes, even before their title says they're ready.

This crossing is about conscious self-advocacy. Not the polite kind where you wait for permission to be brilliant. The kind where you recognize your own clarity and start acting like it matters.

That thing you named at the start of this chapter? The one sitting in your chest? Here's your first question: **Have you chosen to move on it, or are you still waiting for permission?**

That's your signal. Stop apologizing for receiving it.

The Authority Scatter

Want to know how we kill our own agency? We scatter our authority like we're feeding pigeons. "What do you think?" "Do you approve?" "Should I maybe consider possibly..."

Stop. This isn't collaboration. It's death by a thousand permissions.

Writing this book, I've been ruthless about seeking editorial feedback while never asking for opinions on whether I *should* write it. One sharpens the execution; the other outsources your spine.

You might have been taught to doubt your intelligence while others were taught to trust theirs. Guess which group still runs the meeting?

The Voice That Keeps You Circling

The first resistance isn't out there. It's that whisper in your own head, muttering you're not credentialed enough, experienced enough, polished enough to make this move.

Listen closely: that voice gets louder the closer you get to something that matters. It's not protecting you from failure. **It's protecting you from disrupting what's comfortable.**

Your clarity was never the problem. The problem was a system that needed you to doubt it.

Action: The Second Crossing

Behavior (noun)

What you do when you think no one important is paying attention, including you. And since "important" is subjective, let's be honest, some of us made strangers' opinions matter way too much. Time to stop that.

Behavior is the lived expression of your choices, the real-time proof of what you value versus what you profess to value.

To Express (verb)

To stop hiding behind good intentions and start making your choices visible enough that others can judge whether you mean what you say.

So, you've claimed your agency and made conscious choices. Congratulations. Now comes the part that separates insight from impact, **bringing that choice into the world where people can watch you either nail it or completely flame out.**

This is where your credibility gets its stress test. Where what you say you believe and how you move get to meet each other in broad daylight. No script. No do-overs. Just you, your choices, and everyone taking detailed notes on whether you mean it.

The Values Fraud Detection System

Your values aren't what you put on the website. They're what you do when nobody's keeping score. When the budget gets tight. When the pressure mounts. When someone disagrees with you in front of the whole team.

You say you value courage, then send a passive-aggressive email the second someone disagrees. You preach "fail forward" then run post-mortems like a team-building retreat hosted by your worst ex. You post about equity, but your hires still look like your golf league.

Congratulations, you just destroyed your credibility faster than a wellness influencer caught eating fast food.

Yeah, that's where your words and your behavior finally make eye contact. And it's about as comfortable as running into your therapist at the grocery store while buying wine and ice cream.

I've seen "trust and transparency" etched into company values like commandments, while real decisions happen in side chats and private calendars. The same leaders who brag about open-door policies somehow manage to keep those doors sealed tighter than a vault when accountability comes knocking.

And those self-proclaimed "values champions"? Some of them save their darkest behavior for when no one's watching.

The truth: The gap between what we claim and what we do isn't just hypocrisy. It's organizational poison. It seeps into culture, corrodes credibility, and teaches everyone to stop believing words altogether. Innovation withers because who risks honesty in a place that punishes it? Trust evaporates faster than morning dew in August.

When Someone Finally Drops the Act

The merger was brutal. When the new VP arrived, everyone was primed to hate him. It had the same energy as meeting a parent's new partner and you've already decided they're the worst? That energy filled every hallway conversation.

He inherited a culture built on hoarding information and closed-door decisions. His first leadership meeting could've been another round of corporate karaoke about synergy and alignment.

Instead, he pulled the chairs into a circle and asked every leader to name their last major decision and who it impacted.

Silence. Heavy. Uncomfortable. He didn't fill it. He waited.

"I approved a software budget that's going to make engineering miserable," one director finally admitted.

"I killed a promotion because I was scared, they'd outgrow us," said another.

One by one, the truth started flowing. Not perfect truth. Not polished truth. Just truth about real decisions with real consequences.

Three weeks later, something remarkable happened. People were naming their decisions before making them. Asking who would be affected. The honesty had gone viral.

Real change never starts with a policy. It starts when someone finally tells the truth and stays in the room long enough to prove it's safe.

The Gap That Destroys Everything

Here's the question that makes everyone's palms sweat. If someone shadowed you for a week and watched your real choices, your unfiltered reactions, your 2 A.M. stress decisions, what would they say you value?

The distance between that answer and what's on your professional profile? That's not just your work. That's the crater where your leadership credibility used to live.

That's the abyss Nietzsche was going on about.

We all have that gap. The question isn't whether you're a fraud. The question is whether you're brave enough to close it before it swallows your entire culture whole.

Here's what's coming. The future belongs to leaders who can't be separated from their values. Younger generations have built-in authenticity detectors that make airport security look amateur. They'll spot performative leadership from three departments away.

Fair warning. Alignment makes people nervous.

The moment your behavior starts matching your choices and values, resistance shows up disguised as helpful concern. "Maybe we should roll this out more slowly." Translation: "Please stop making us uncomfortable by meaning what you say."

This resistance feels personal because it is. Your integrity threatens their comfortable dysfunction.

Stand anyway. Act anyway. Close the gap anyway.

The future is watching. And it's taking notes.

Capacity: The Third Crossing

Capacity (noun)

Your readiness to hold more complexity, uncertainty, and responsibility without your nervous system staging a full revolt. The space between what you can handle today and what terrifies you just enough to be interesting.

To Expand (verb)

To step into bigger spaces because you're ready to fill them, not because someone with a performance improvement plan told you to grow or else.

This crossing changes everything. If you breezed through the first two, congratulations. Now comes the moment your comfort zone packs its bags and leaves without forwarding its address.

Feel that hesitation when someone asks you to take on something bigger? That's not imposter syndrome. That's your system recognizing the edge of growth. Most people treat that signal like a stop sign. The Curious treat it like a green light.

Growth and stretch aren't the same animal. Growth makes you better at what you already do. Stretch builds the capacity to hold complexity that would've sent last year's version of you straight to the anxiety Olympics.

Who Are You Now?

I was 42 when I realized I'd been performing someone else's version of *successful adult* for decades.

The career looked good on paper. The credentials were impressive. The life checked all the boxes.

And I was suffocating.

Then came the late diagnoses, autism, and ADHD. Suddenly all the things I'd been told were "too much" or "too intense" made sense.

Sorry about that whole gifted-kid detour, said the system. Turns out I was gifted *and* feral.

Once I saw it, I couldn't unsee it. I didn't want to mask anymore. I didn't want to play small to stay palatable. I wanted to serve and spark tough conversations in my own wild way, which meant building my own nature preserve and running it on *intuition, improvisation,* and *inclusion*. Yes, my three strongest Seeds.

The version of me that said yes to everything, that contorted into whatever shape the room needed, that prioritized everyone's comfort over my own clarity? She had to go.

She wasn't wrong. I'd outgrown her.

The moment you realize the identity everyone expects you to maintain no longer fits is disorienting. The relationships, the role, the routines that once felt right start to feel like shoes two sizes too small.

That's not a crisis. That's expansion asking for permission to happen.

The hardest part wasn't deciding to change. It was disappointing the people who preferred the outdated version, the one who didn't ask tough questions, who didn't challenge comfortable assumptions, who stayed small enough to manage.

Capacity isn't about handling more work. **It's about becoming someone who can hold the truth of who you are becoming, even when it makes other people deeply uncomfortable.**

The Perfectionism Trap

While you're polishing that strategy until it could blind astronauts, the world's out there lapping you. While you wait for the perfect moment to speak up, someone else is making decisions that change lives. While you're sculpting the flawless approach, the problems multiply and your team starts giving you that face.

Me, with this book, right up to the 11th hour. If Dropbox had feelings, it would be pacing the hallway at 11:59 p.m.

You know that face. **Stop. Just stop.**

I've been that person, AM that person. Orbiting brilliant ideas like abandoned satellites, never quite ready to launch. Collecting "in development" files while opportunities sprint past like they're late for dinner. Oh, the ideas collecting on my desk.

Perfectionism isn't polish. It's fear in a productivity costume, nervously clutching the pearls of a task list.

That discomfort you're experiencing? It's not a malfunction. It's your internal compass recalibrating, guiding you directly toward the next version of yourself who is equipped to handle the challenges ahead.

Your Next Move

Where's life tapping you on the shoulder right now? What chance keeps circling back, whispering, *You could do this... if you'd stop waiting to feel ready?*

That discomfort isn't your enemy. It's your growth detector, more accurate than any performance review, more honest than your inner critic. The fact that you can feel it means you're already standing at the threshold.

Ready is a myth sold by people who profit from your hesitation. Willing is what gets you across.

Trust what you know. Stretch anyway.

Knowledge: The Fourth Crossing

Competency (noun)

Knowledge that's been tested in the real world and lived to talk about it. The practiced expression of what you know, strengthened by everything you've learned in the first three crossings.

To Apply (verb)

To set what you know into motion through grounded presence, aligned action, and expanded capacity. Application happens when all four crossings converge, transforming knowledge into impact.

You know that moment when the smartest person in the meeting makes everyone else feel like furniture? When brilliant analysis somehow makes the actual problem worse? When expertise becomes a weapon instead of a tool?

That's knowledge without the other crossings. And we've all been collateral damage.

Here's what makes me want to yell into the forest: we keep promoting people for what they *know* instead of how they *show up*. Handing leadership roles to technical stars who leave human wreckage behind like it's the cost of doing business. We celebrate outputs and ignore the broken relationships quietly labeled "organizational roadkill."

Then we stand around, baffled, wondering why engagement keeps tanking even as metrics sparkle. DDI's *Global Leadership Forecast 2025* puts it bluntly: "Trust in immediate managers dropped from 46% to 29%."[3] The immediate manager.

Being the smartest person in the room means nothing if you can't make conscious choices, align your behavior, or stretch beyond what's comfortable.

Give me someone with strong agency, authentic action, and genuine capacity over a brilliant extractor any day.

Your culture can't survive extraction. Count on it.

When Expertise Skips the Line

Here's what happens when you jump straight to knowledge without crossing the other three:

Knowledge without agency is compliance wearing a lab coat. You execute flawlessly but couldn't explain why it matters if your life depended on it.

Knowledge without action is performance art. All analysis, zero follow-through. Beautiful presentations, broken promises.

Knowledge without capacity is controlled chaos. Decisions get made, actions get taken, but nobody owns what happens when it all goes sideways.

The brilliant bulldozers who think emotional intelligence is for everyone else, so people can tolerate their genius. They can solve any technical problem but somehow make everyone around them fantasize about career changes.

When someone delivers results while creating harm, you face a choice that reveals everything about your values. Your team is watching, taking notes on what you protect: the work or the people doing it.

The Knowledge Fortress Problem

Be honest: are you using your expertise as a security blanket, a little wubbie of wisdom, to avoid the messy business of showing up as human?

Here's where it gets sneaky. Some of the biggest, most dangerous resistance in your culture comes dressed in professionalism and wrapped in credentials.

We dismiss connection as "soft skills," like they're optional extras. Meanwhile, culture crumbles because nobody can collaborate, speak honestly, or trust each other enough to take real risks.

Sometimes the person, the problem, the leader...is us.

What would happen if you stopped hiding behind what you know and started leading with who you are?

You were taught that being right matters more than being connected. That intelligence excuses impact. That expertise grants exemptions from basic human decency.

When you see pages of creative ideas, innovative work, and enthusiastic faces, do you feel that irresistible urge to point out the one tiny error with a cutting comment about "attention to detail"?

Congratulations. You've just valued competency over connection.

The future belongs to people who can't be separated from their values, who use knowledge as a bridge, not a wall.

Time to build bridges.

Standing on the Other Side

Look at you. You've crossed every threshold that separates people who talk about leadership from people who live it. Agency, Action, Capacity, Knowledge.

You're not the same person who started this chapter. You've got language now for what you've been sensing all along. There will be moments you feel anything but ready. *Willing* will carry you every single time. Ready is overrated anyway. It's often just performative certainty wearing a fancy outfit to the party.

Willing is different. Willing is real. Willing lives in the moment and says, "yes, even though my knees are shaking." Deep resolve in your willingness will always outlast a shaky version of readiness.

When you fully commit to your own presence in the world, everything shifts. The crossings are a living practice that gets tested every single time you walk into a room where decisions get made. Every time you must choose between looking professional and being human.

When the Performance Ends

Presence reveals itself when the mask slips and nobody's clapping. When you have to admit you don't know something in front of people who think you should. When your voice shakes and you say what needs saying.

That's not weakness showing. That's your stance revealing itself. The foundation that holds when everything else feels like shifting sand.

Your performance review will never capture this moment. There's no metric for choosing truth over comfort or connection over compliance. But your team will remember. They'll remember the day you let go of certainty and started practicing presence.

The Secret About Solo Acts

Here's something that'll make you reconsider everything: these crossings don't happen in isolation. Every guide needs a forest. Every sustainable breakthrough happens in community. The crossings we just mapped? They multiply in power when you're not crossing them alone.

Think about it. The last time you made a decision that truly mattered, who had your back? Who saw what you were trying to build before you could name it yourself? Who held space for your messy process without trying to manage or fix it?

That's not coincidence. That's architecture. The invisible networks that decide whether your courage takes root or gets choked out by systems built for comfort.

The forest can't make the crossing for you. It can steady you, witness you, hold you in community, remind you you're not alone. But it can't say yes on your behalf. The willingness has to come from inside you. The decision is always yours.

Which brings us to the underground systems that make everything we've covered sustainable. Our last part of Emerging is the Mycelia of Inclusion: those vast, invisible networks that connect and nourish entire ecosystems.

Just like in forests, the real magic happens below ground. Damage these networks and everything above eventually dies, no matter how impressive individual performance looks on paper.

You've been building these networks without knowing it. Every time you redirected credit where it belonged. Every conversation where you chose to understand instead of being understood. Every moment you used your position to lift instead of hoard.

Time to see what you've been growing in the dark.

[3] DDI, *Global Leadership Forecast 2025*.

SIGNAL CHECK

SELF

What's the one thing you <u>know</u> but are not doing right now, and what would it take to move from *choosing it* to *doing it*, even if your knees are shaking?

TEAM

As a team, where have we been waiting for permission or certainty before moving forward, and what becomes possible when we choose willing over ready?

CULTURE

Looking at how we develop and promote leaders, what would shift if we valued agency, aligned action, and expanded capacity as much as we value technical expertise and credentials?

CHAPTER FOUR: THE ETHOS OF RECLAMATION

Five

The Mycelia of Inclusion

Belonging · Community · Sustainability

You walk into a room, and your radar starts *screaming*. Before you can name what's wrong, you've catalogued every micro-aggression, every power play, every desperate attempt to look inclusive while being anything but.

Conversations die when leadership shows up. Values posters cover up decisions made in bathrooms by people who went to the same schools, live in the same zip codes, vacation in the same places.

They're measuring psychological safety while you're calculating how much truth you can afford this quarter.

Your stomach does that thing it does when you smell gas but can't find the leak. Something's wrong here. Something's been wrong for a while. But everyone's smiling and nodding like this is totally normal, totally fine, totally not the place where promising ideas go to die slow, bureaucratic deaths.

You know why? Because you've been doing ecosystem analysis in every environment throughout your life without knowing it. Reading invisible networks, tracking resource flows, mapping who gets fed and who gets forgotten. Your pattern recognition is so sharp it makes meteorologists jealous.

The organizations surviving the next disruption? They're figuring out ecosystemic leadership right now.

Every thriving forest runs on underground networks that would make our leadership structures weep with embarrassment. Mycelia. Fungal threads connecting everything, shuttling nutrients from abundance to scarcity, composting death into life, building resilience that would make our best systems architects quit their jobs and become mushroom farmers.

These networks don't just move resources. They redistribute them. A tree struggling in shade gets sugars from the one standing in sun. Nutrients flow toward need, not hierarchy. The strongest trees don't hoard; they share. Because when one part of the network fails, the whole system becomes vulnerable.

Poison this underground web? Those gorgeous trees keep standing for months, fooling everyone into thinking the forest thrives right up until the whole ecosystem face-plants spectacularly.

Fix them? *Life explodes back so fast you'll think someone hit fast-forward.*

Your workplace? Your neighborhood association? Your activist collective? Same game, different players. Invisible networks decide who hears about opportunities first, who gets introduced to actual power versus sent to networking seminars, who receives backup when pressure mounts.

Never what you see above ground. Always what's been protected or destroyed below. Behind closed doors. *Offline.*

Organizations strip-mine their own talent while wondering why innovation dies. Building culture decks while systematically destroying the conditions leadership needs to survive, operating extraction systems that would make mining companies blush.

You cannot build what you will not tend. You cannot tend what you refuse to nourish.

The 3 Rs: Recognition, Restoration, and Reverence

Time to map the invisible architecture running your life while you focused on quarterly metrics and performance reviews.

Three skills for ecosystemic leadership. Not another framework to implement. Not steps to follow. These are survival skills for reading what's happening beneath every polished surface.

Recognition sees the networks beneath the surface. Who's feeding whom. Where nutrients flow. What's choking out growth while everyone applauds the flowers.

Restoration kills what's strangling life and plants what serves it. Composting dead systems. Protecting what grows. Sometimes that means walking away from soil too poisoned to save.

Reverence tends ground where others flourish without needing your name on anything. The work is the point. The connection is the outcome.

This works *everywhere*. Fortune 500 boardrooms. Parent-teacher conferences. Neighborhood associations. Your activist collective. Your family dynamics.

Soil is soil. Either nutrients flow or they don't. Either connections strengthen or they atrophy.

No middle ground. No neutral territory.

You're either feeding the ecosystem or the it's feeding on you.

Recognition: What The Curious Already Know

Your instincts about that toxic workplace? Dead right. *Always have been.* But try explaining invisible power networks to someone whose biggest workplace challenge is remembering which parking spot is theirs.

What invisible networks? Jerry from accounting treats everyone the same!

Sure. If you're the *right* definition of friendly. The *right* team player. If you laugh at the *right* jokes and stay quiet during the wrong conversations.

You clock who gets real information before the announcement drops. You watch brilliant ideas get buried until Brad from Strategy resurrects them as "disruptive innovation" and gets a corner office. You notice who carries emotional labor and who gets rewarded for "natural leadership ability." You see which questions get explored and which ones get people labeled "not a culture fit."

Some people pay rent just to occupy space in these systems. Others inherited the keys.

Most networks weren't built by bond villains plotting world domination. They're maintained by perfectly lovely humans who genuinely believe the best ideas win, completely oblivious that their idea-detection software only recognizes certain frequencies.

Map out the course of this situation and then decide your next move.

Your Detective Assignment

Want to see what's flowing through your system? Detective time. Grab your metaphorical magnifying glass and comfortable shoes.

Follow the Real Money: For one week, track who knows about opportunities before they're posted. Whose pet projects get funding while others die in budget purgatory. At your kid's school, notice which parent gets the principal's cell number versus which ones fill out the online form that disappears into the void. Who ends up managing everyone's meltdowns when deadlines explode or the fundraiser implodes.

Just observe. Don't fix. Most people get whiplash when they see the difference between what the org chart says and how resources move. A moment of awareness, it's challenging to see it clearly for the first time.

Shadow the Shadow Meetings: Real decisions happen over lunch, during school pickup, in group texts you didn't know existed, at the coffee shop after the official meeting ends. Map who's in those conversations. Who gets advance warning about the reorganization, the school boundary changes, the budget cuts. Who finds out when the memo drops, or the email blast goes out.

Chart the Safety Zones: Psychological safety isn't distributed like municipal water. It pools in specific places, often around specific people. Whose questions spark curiosity versus damage control? Who can push back without wondering if they'll still have a job next month, a seat at the table next quarter, an invitation next time? Make sure you're not asking folks to be brave, loud, feral without a safety net under them.

You already know what you're going to find. You've known for months, maybe... years. The question isn't whether you're ready to see it. It's what you'll do once you can't unsee it.

The Cost of Invisible Extraction

Here's your story, isn't it? You spot icebergs while everyone else admires the cruise ship. You connect dots that won't officially connect until consulting firms get paid six figures to draw the same lines. You ask questions that make rooms go quiet because they point at elephants everyone agreed to ignore.

What happens to your insights? Filed under "thanks for your input" until someone with an Ivy League degree says *exactly the same thing* and gets hailed as a visionary.

This isn't about your bruised ego, though watching someone get promoted off your ideas stings like hell. This is about organizations that systematically waste their own intelligence. They miss market shifts, botch crisis responses, make expensive mistakes while information that could save them sits dismissed in the wrong person's mouth.

McKinsey's research found that companies in the top quartile for ethnic and cultural diversity outperformed those in the bottom quartile by 36 percent in profitability.[4]

Eventually, you leave. They act *shocked* when competitors snap you up and suddenly start making moves, they should have seen coming from orbit.

That's extraction in action. Systems that take without feeding back don't just burn people out. They damage their own evolutionary capacity. When disruption hits, they can't adapt because they trained their smartest sensors to stop sending signals.

Recognition means seeing systems as they operate, not as they perform in annual reports. Real inclusion isn't measured by diversity photos. It's whether different perspectives can change what happens, not just witness what happens.

The most dangerous phrase in organizational life? "**We value all voices.**" Meant well, but without follow-through and commitment, it's the biggest of lies.

Restoration: From Diagnosis to Action

If extraction is the disease, restoration is the cure. Not through another diversity training or wellness Wednesday, but through deliberately changing how resources, opportunity, and support move through your systems.

Sometimes leadership means looking at a broken system and saying: this dies today. Composting. Free those resources to feed something else.

A nonprofit director realized their mentorship program was nepotism wearing social justice makeup. White, cisgender, educated staff had invisible champions while everyone else got motivational posters about "believing in yourself." She could have launched another task force to study mentorship equity gaps.

Instead? Monthly storytelling circles. Space for people to share real experiences across departments. Three months later, staff were building mentorship networks based on genuine connection rather than resume pedigree.

She didn't create innovation. **She created conditions where innovation could thrive.**

That's the shift most systems miss entirely.

The Art of Strategic Death

Restoration starts with a decision that makes nice people break out in nervous sweats: some structures must die before healthy ones can grow.

That meeting where three people hold court while everyone else mentally writes grocery lists? *Kill it.* The approval chain requiring six signatures for office supplies? *Dead.* The hiring committee "seeking culture fit" while mysteriously passing on every candidate who doesn't golf?

Time. To. Compost.

Broken systems have fierce defenders. People who built careers around being essential bottlenecks. They'll lecture you about "maintaining standards" and "preserving institutional knowledge."

Translation: My paycheck depends on keeping this dysfunction breathing.

Restoration means disappointing people who profit from broken systems. *Get comfortable with that feeling.*

Pick one structure strangling something beautiful. The budget process treating a $50 expense like a mortgage application. The committee "thoughtfully deliberating" the same decision since the last presidential election.

Don't improve it. Don't optimize it. Don't hire consultants to study it.

Kill it cleanly and build something that serves the work instead of feeding egos.

Then protect what grows with everything you have. Old systems regenerate faster than weeds the moment you're not watching.

When Someone Does Surgery

A department head inherited a team where information crawled at bureaucratic speed and credit flowed upward to whoever had the nicest office. She could have called this "organizational culture" and managed the dysfunction.

Instead, she performed surgery on the system itself.

Killed weekly status meetings where nothing got decided. Started sharing budget numbers her boss hoarded like state secrets. Began redirecting praise to whoever did the work instead of whoever claimed credit later.

Her boss called it "a threat to proven processes." Her team called it the first real leadership they'd experienced in years.

Six months later? Crushing every performance metric while working reasonable hours.

The difference? She'd stopped feeding the extraction machine and planted something that grew.

Your systems will eventually need composting. The only question is whether you'll participate consciously or wait for everything to collapse and force your hand.

Which sounds like more fun?

Reverence: The Steward's Path

I've spent decades protecting spaces that were never designed for me.

Protecting space for each other is how we make room for everyone's way of being so we can all breathe, think, and exist without translation.

Living in the margins of neurodivergence, queerness, and womanhood taught me to guard those margins for others too: Black and Brown people, trans and nonbinary folk, anyone still navigating systems that mistake oppression for order.

The margins sharpen your senses. You learn what's safe, what's performance, and what still carries the quiet sting of exclusion, even when it arrives wrapped in good intention.

Systems that process brilliant humans into corporate drones. Meetings where the sharpest insights come from whoever's been invisible until they finally snap. Hiring committees swearing they want "innovation" while only finding talent from their CEO's alumni directory.

Boston Consulting Group discovered that organizations with diverse leadership see innovation revenue 19 percentage points higher than companies with below-average diversity.[5] The business case isn't just solid. It's screaming.

Once you see extraction wearing a diversity costume, you can't unsee it. Can't return to nodding through "bring your whole self to work" retreats while everyone performs their most digestible quarter-self.

Navigating this work when your identity shifts between marginalized and privileged depending on which room you're in: it's exhausting in ways nobody warns you about. I'm neurodivergent and queer, which locks me out of some spaces. I'm also white and cisgender, which opens doors others can't see exist.

Staying conscious and open to feedback and growth? Advanced level stuff.

Most of us are walking contradictions. You might be the only woman at the executive table while benefiting from every other systemic advantage. You might champion racial equity while your organization quietly destroys disabled employees.

The work isn't perfect allyship. It's navigating contradictions without causing more damage through good intentions.

And when I see racism playing out in public spaces, on social media, in professional settings? I wade in with my white privilege leading. Every single time. I don't care if it's a stranger. If they cared enough to make it public, I care enough to correct it and speak out. That's what the privilege is for. Absorbing blows that would land harder on people with less protection.

It costs me. Relationships, comfort, professional connections. But this isn't about what it costs me. It's about using whatever unearned advantages I have to shift how power moves.

Pro Tip: Stop DM'ing me, "Don't you think..." when you're asking me not to speak up for myself or others.

The Hidden Work of Inclusion

The real work of inclusion happens when no one's watching. When there's no recognition. When it costs you something.

Redirecting credit to who deserves it, knowing they won't remember you at promotion time. Challenging hiring rejections when candidates are qualified but make people "uncomfortable." Creating space for steamrolled voices while stepping back yourself.

But watch what happens when people doing this work don't get expected recognition. Suddenly it's "*I built this place! I bled for this! Where's my throne?*"

That's when protection becomes performance wearing social justice clothing.

Inclusion doesn't work through transactions. You don't trade protection for authority. You tend soil you'll never harvest. **You plant trees whose shade will cool strangers.**

The forest doesn't thank mycelial networks. The work is the point; the connection is the outcome.

Creating Microclimates Where Humans Can Breathe

You don't need corner-office authority to change how power moves. You can create pockets of sanity within systems that seem designed by people who think feelings are performance issues.

This is where Recognition, Restoration, and Reverence converge into something you can use Monday morning. You map patterns in your immediate sphere. You kill what's toxic where you have influence. You protect conditions for others without needing your name on the building.

This week's quiet rebellion:

- Kill one pointless meeting. Tell people it died of natural causes. I wrote an obituary for "Reply All" and sent it to an entire department. *It died.* Stop weaponizing it to invoke authority or credibility.

- Redirect credit in real time. Name the source. *Out loud.*
- Share opportunities with overlooked people. Be the bridge.
- Stop feeding toxic systems. Don't forward poison. Don't laugh at jokes that punch down.

This month's revolution:

- Build information networks serving people, not power.
- Create mutual protection with trusted colleagues.
- Document invisible labor. Make emotional work visible.

These aren't team-building exercises. They're strategic rebellion reshaping power one interaction at a time.

Application: Where Are You Rooting?

Stop scrolling. You. Yes, you. Look around. What soil are you trying to grow in right now?

Your nervous system has been filing reports for months, and you keep explaining them away with logic that would make philosophers weep. No matter how brilliant you are, how many workshops you attend, or how much kombucha you drink, **you cannot thrive in poisoned ground.**

You can white-knuckle it for a while. But eventually, even the most resilient plants die in toxic soil.

Are you dumping your best ideas into organizations that treat innovation like a suggestion box they check quarterly? Pretzel-twisting yourself to fit into spaces designed by someone who can't mention "DEI" without a sneer? Performing gratitude for scraps while your brain screams "*I could run this place better in my sleep*"?

Your body's been keeping score. Those stress dreams about work? The way your jaw clenches when certain names appear in your calendar? The Sunday evening dread settling in your chest like fog?

That's not anxiety. That's intelligence.

The Brutal Inventory

Apply Recognition to your own ecosystem.

Ask yourself where you've been accepting extraction as the cost of having a seat at the table.

Notice when your shoulders migrate toward your ears before meetings. Track which conversations leave you feeling like someone siphoned out your life force with a straw. Pay attention to environments where you shrink versus expand like you've been holding your breath for decades.

Think about the last time you felt *genuinely alive* at work. Not caffeinated or productive. **Alive.** What made that possible? Who was in the room? How did decisions happen?

Now for the part that'll make you want to close this book: **Notice how you participate in your own depletion.** When do you apologize before sharing insights that could save everyone time and money? When do you accept behavior that would make your teenager say, "*that's not normal, Mom*"?

Where are you nodding yes while every cell votes no?

The Liberation Math

Sometimes the most powerful act of restoration and reverence is walking away. This isn't failure or abandonment. It's ecological wisdom. Just as certain plants can't survive in depleted soil no matter how much they adapt, some environments cannot, or will not, support your strengths.

Some soil is beyond restoration. Some cultures would rather hemorrhage talent than examine why talented people keep leaving. Systems so committed to broken patterns they'll sacrifice their best people to protect their worst habits.

I know leaders who spent years thinking they were the problem. If they just tried harder, spoke softer, got one more certification, they'd finally thrive in environments designed to extract rather than cultivate. (*It's me. And others, but also, me.*) Their breakthrough came when they stopped fixing themselves for places that were never going to value what they brought.

When they found soil that could support their growth, they didn't just survive. **They exploded into the leaders they'd always been** under all that coping fatigue.

Your internal warning system doesn't lie. When it consistently tells you a place extracts more than it gives, *believe it.*

I know some of you are thinking: "Must be nice to have options." Economic constraints, visa status, caregiving responsibilities. The privilege of choosing better soil isn't equally distributed. When leaving isn't possible, the work becomes building protective boundaries while creating underground networks of mutual support.

This isn't just survival. It's resistance that gradually transforms conditions from within.

What would change if you treated soil health as seriously as performance metrics?

As We Move Forward

You've restored your own soil. Learned to recognize when nutrients flow versus when extraction dominates. You understand how underground networks determine what survives above ground.

You've composted what was strangling your growth. Planted what serves life. Tended ground where others can flourish without needing your name carved into anything.

But ecosystems don't thrive in isolation.

The work you've done, this rewilding of your own leadership, this return to trusting what you know and who you are beneath all the performance scripts? That's the foundation.

You've been learning to be a steward of your own ground.

Now we explore what it means to steward entire ecosystems together.

In the next section, your individual Guideship and Signal meets others who've done their own restoration work. Where the networks you've been tending start connecting to adjacent systems. Where the microclimates you've been protecting in your sphere start influencing entire ecosystems and ask: what becomes possible when connections form?

When your way of moving through the world meets someone else's, and together you reshape how power flows through entire cultures?

This is about collective restoration. Multiple leaders who've stopped performing and started trusting their pattern recognition. Teams that have learned to spot extraction and choose nourishment instead. Organizations rewilding themselves back to conditions where brilliance doesn't have to hide.

In the ecology of guideship, ecotones create what isolated systems cannot. These transition zones, where different approaches meet and interact, offer a higher diversity of thought, greater density of innovation, unique solutions that emerge only at the boundaries.

The richest leadership happens in these zones of active exchange.

You've built the foundation. Now let's enter the bigger systems.

Chapter 5 Endnotes:

[4] McKinsey & Company, *Diversity Wins: How Inclusion Matters* (2020). Companies in the top quartile for ethnic and cultural diversity on executive teams were 36 percent more likely to outperform on profitability than those in the fourth quartile.

[5] Boston Consulting Group, *How Diverse Leadership Teams Boost Innovation* (2018). Companies with above-average diversity on management teams reported innovation revenue 19 percentage points higher than companies with below-average leadership

SIGNAL CHECK

SELF

What are the invisible networks in your organization already telling you about who gets nourished and who doesn't, and what would restoration look like in the sphere where you have influence?

TEAM

As a team, where do we see nutrients flowing toward <u>need</u> versus flowing toward <u>hierarchy</u>, and what would it take to redistribute resources, opportunities, and support more intentionally?

CULTURE

Looking across the organization, what would shift if we treated inclusion as the mycelia that feeds everything else, not a program to run, but the underground network that determines whether innovation, trust, and adaptability can survive?

The Confluence
From Guide to Ecosystems

Six

The Collective Strategic Mind

Signal Intelligence for Strategy and Teams

The first time I recognized true Signal Intelligence in action, I almost missed it.

I was facilitating a quarterly review for a mid-sized tech company. Everything seemed perfect on paper. Revenue projections? Hit. Customer retention? Steady. Growth? Modest but consistent. It was the meeting where executives relax, close laptops with satisfying snaps, and congratulate each other.

Yet beneath the self-congratulation, something was missing.

The operations director felt it too. She'd been quiet during the celebration, and as the CEO wrapped up with remarks about "staying the course," she set down her pen deliberately.

"I think we're solving yesterday's problem," she said. Her words hit like a stone into still water. "Our customers are telling us something our dashboards can't see yet."

The CEO looked up, curiosity replacing satisfaction. "You think there's a market shift coming?"

"It's already here," she replied. "We're just not feeling it yet."

She shared what she'd noticed: Customer calls running longer, questions growing more complex, sales cycles stretching, support tickets asking about integrations once dismissed as unimportant. None of this showed up in formal reports. These were patterns she'd observed while walking the floors, listening to calls, and reading between the lines of customer emails.

Three months later, when their biggest competitor launched a platform addressing the shift she'd sensed, her company wasn't scrambling. They were already evolving. They didn't have better data. They listened to the signal before it became noise.

This wasn't dumb luck or random gut instinct.

This was Signal Intelligence: the ability to read patterns before they fully form and act decisively while others wait for certainty.

Intuition and improvisation were in play.

Guideship changes everything.

From Personal Signal to Organizational Force

You've reclaimed your edges, felt the tremor of intention, cultivated Seeds of Potential that ground your leadership. You've embodied Guideship, allowing movement without domination. You've felt your Signal emerge, that authentic current of leadership flowing through you.

Now we turn outward.

From individual to collective. From personal practice to organizational impact. From the Signal within you to Signal Intelligence transforming systems. The practices work whether you lead an entire organization or just yourself. Each begins with personal development, then extends outward to create team and organizational impact.

Your personal Signal can't scale without becoming a distributed capacity. When cultivated, it transforms how organizations sense, interpret, and respond to reality.

When I burned out from being the sole nervous system in my organization, spotting every pattern but keeping it to myself, I learned this the hard way. It's like installing a single smoke detector in a 50-story building. One person sensing everything is exhausting. A whole organization sensing together? That's power.

Signal Intelligence is in play even as I write this book. For years, I hesitated to share these ideas because I don't hold a doctorate. I feared my voice would be dismissed without academic credentials. I watched countless leadership books emerge (some excellent, some merely recycling old ideas) and felt the tension between what I sensed and what I didn't say.

But here's what I recognized: this isn't an academic tome. It's a distillation of nearly 30 years in the people space, consulting across sectors, working with leaders at conferences and summits, and thousands of hours in coaching. I am deeply educated and experienced. I needed to believe in my own feral capacity and walk as a guide.

What I've consistently observed is a pattern: leaders who sense shifts early, maintain direction amid chaos, foster connection under pressure, and find creative openings consistently outperform those with impressive credentials but undeveloped perception.

That pattern, impossible to ignore even when traditional authority advised silence, led me to trust my Signal. To apply Signal Intelligence with my Guideship, trusting its resonance.

It shifts the fundamental leadership question from "How do I get people to see what I see?" to "How do we collectively sense what's emerging before it's obvious?"

And "How do we make it the norm instead of the exception?"

What Becomes Possible

Here's what I love about Signal Intelligence: it doesn't prevent disasters. It creates capacity.

When this comprehension flows through an organization, you're building foresight. You're expanding the window of choice. You're creating space to respond before pressure force's reaction.

You know that feeling when you wake slightly off, and by mid-afternoon you're sick? You had a window. A moment when rest might have changed everything. Organizations have those windows too. Signal Intelligence helps you find them.

One of my favorite metaphors, in a Grey's Anatomy way, is to picture a body with a damaged nervous system that only registers pain after severe damage has occurred. That's what happens in companies waiting for lagging indicators to confirm what people sensed months ago: markets shifting, talent disengaging, operations fracturing. We're moving ahead of the pressure.

You don't need heroic interventions. Well, you might, and we'll get there, but you start now and keep building.

We're looking for moments where perception meets timely action, before external pressure demands it. The greatest successes of Signal Intelligence often appear as non-events. Crises that never materialize. Talent that remains loyal. Opportunities seized so smoothly they seem inevitable.

This is what you're building. It's not a prediction machine. It is a team, function, or entire organization that senses and responds to emerging realities while action still feels optional.

Where Signal Intelligence Shows Up

You already know where the gaps are. Strategy built on last year's data. Culture measured once a quarter while your best people quietly disengage. Operations held together by workarounds nobody talks about.

Signal Intelligence doesn't add more systems. It helps you see what's already happening before it shows up in the reports.

Strategy: Seeing the Shift Before the Data Confirms It

I've sat through countless strategy sessions where teams dissect historical data, hoping another slice will somehow reveal the future. I've done it myself. Commissioned the analysis, demanded more granularity, extended the trend lines. As if perfect hindsight creates foresight.

You know the pattern. Organizations create strategies that quietly become outdated. By the time market shifts appear in the usual indicators, everyone's scrambling.

Trust what your frontline teams hear. When customer language shifts, when prospects ask unexpected questions, when implementation hits friction in unfamiliar places, those aren't anomalies. They're signals.

Now give your team permission to share what they're noticing.

Culture: Feeling the Current Before People Leave

I made this mistake leading a team early in my career. We had all the cultural initiatives, surveys, town halls, open doors. Yet I missed the shift until three key members resigned within a week. The exit interviews revealed issues building for months that no one felt safe raising. The surveys said we were fine. Our culture wasn't.

You've seen this. The sudden resignation that wasn't sudden. The exit interview surfacing problems everyone already knew but nobody said aloud.

A professional services firm faced this after losing several key people in quick succession. Instead of panic-hiring or throwing money at retention, they started informal monthly check-ins. Not about projects or task lists, but about how it felt to work there.

Within two months, they'd spotted something the annual survey never caught: tension between stated work-life balance values and the implicit expectation of constant availability. It showed up in small ways. Who spoke in meetings and who'd gone quiet. Which conversations happened in hallways versus text. The informal networks dissolving.

They addressed it through behavior changes, not policy updates. Leaders modeled different availability patterns. They made space for candid conversation about the gap between what they said and what they rewarded.

The result? People stayed. The culture strengthened. Meanwhile, competitors with better benefits and higher salaries struggled with turnover.

When team energy shifts, you're usually the first to recognize the moment. When collaboration patterns change. When certain topics create tension. Trust that. Culture isn't abstract, it's the daily patterns you can feel if you're paying attention.

Operations: Catching Friction While It's Still Small

A project unraveled over three months, and I watched it happen. Meetings started five minutes late, then ten, then fifteen. Questions about deliverables multiplied. Small reworks crept in, untracked. Yet the dashboard stayed green because no major milestone had been missed yet. Yet is such a dangerous word in the wrong hands.

When it finally collapsed, everyone claimed shock. "Unforeseen circumstances." Except the circumstances had been signaling for months.

Most operational dysfunction isn't sudden. Teams shift priorities, deadlines slip, and resources stretch. By the time it shows up in the metrics, you're reacting to symptoms, not causes.

A manufacturing company kept hitting the same wall: deadline crises around quality assurance. They'd add more tracking, tighten processes, and demand better estimates. Nothing changed.

Finally, they tried something different. A simple ask. *Where is the friction?*

Feedback is a scary word that spooks people. They hear, "Tell me what I'm doing wrong." Conflict sounds like a fight waiting to happen. But friction? Friction just names what's already there, rubbing against progress. People can answer that.

The pattern appeared at once: they consistently underestimated QA time. The estimators weren't bad at their jobs. The planning templates were structured poorly. One small adjustment transformed a chronic problem into a competitive advantage.

Look at the patterns, the meetings starting late or running over, communication becoming hesitant, the same questions keep coming up, and the unofficial workarounds spreading. They're not isolated incidents. Operations is trying to tell you something. Listen before the dashboard forces you to.

Three Practices For Progress

Signal Intelligence doesn't need elaborate systems or fancy consultants. It needs space, attention, and trust. Here are three practices that work.

Create Space to Notice Together

Most meetings confirm what's already known. Teams update on metrics, known issues, and progress. Important, but not enough.

Start holding regular sessions (weekly for teams, monthly for departments) where the only agenda is: *What are you noticing that doesn't fit our usual patterns?*

The first time I tried this with a leadership team, I asked, "What patterns are you noticing?" and got blank stares. I'd forgotten that noticing needs permission, especially in solution-focused cultures. You'll need a minute to create and sustain psychological safety. So, I got specific: "What customer behavior surprised you this week? What question did someone ask that you didn't expect? Where did something take longer than it should have?"

The conversation opened. When you make space for people to be inquisitive about what's happening instead of reporting what happened, you start seeing what's coming.

You're doing this right when "What are you noticing?" becomes as important as "What are you measuring?" When there's safety to share observations without pressure to immediately solve them.

Monday: In your next team meeting, add ten minutes at the end. Ask: "What surprised you this week?" Just listen. Don't solve. Notice what emerges.

Next week: Hold a 30-minute session focused entirely on emerging patterns. What's shifting in customer language? Team energy? Workflow rhythm? Connect dots across functions.

Next month: Make this a regular practice. Weekly for fast-moving teams, monthly for others. Keep it simple. Keep it conversational. Trust what people notice. That last one? That's the hard one.

Track What Comes Before

You know that feeling when you're checking the weather app while already standing in the rain? We do that in organizations, too. Measuring what already happened while being caught off guard by current events.

Quarterly revenue, customer churn, employee turnover... these metrics show where you've been, not where you're headed. We won't win the race by staring in the rearview mirror.

Ask yourself: what happens *before* the thing we care about? What shifts before customer churn rises? What changes will happen before operational efficiency drops? What patterns precede disengagement?

Then track those signals alongside your usual metrics. This is intentional measurement, not just collecting data because it's easy to count.

A healthcare tech company started tracking the types of questions hospital administrators asked during sales calls. When questions shifted from specific features to broader integration concerns, they recognized a market shift three months before competitors did. They didn't have better data. They were watching what came before.

Monday: Pick one metric that matters to your team. Ask: what do we typically see right before this changes? Start noticing those signals.

Next week: Create a simple way to track early signals. A shared doc. A weekly count. A quick ratio. 1-2 that matter, not 8-10 that create noise. Nothing elaborate. Just visible.

Next month: Use these signals in decision-making. Not as certainty, but as indicators worth exploring. When three customers in the same segment ask for the same thing, that's a signal. When team communication drops in cross-functional meetings, that's a signal. When small delays start repeating, that's a signal.

Connect People Who Don't Usually Talk

Organizations love talking about breaking down silos while reinforcing them through structure, metrics, and incentives. It's like building hallways between rooms but keeping the doors locked.

It reminds me of when my GPS led me through a cow pasture as a "shortcut," much like those "efficient" cross-functional processes that look good on paper but have you wading through... well, not grass. I've seen companies create complex structures and frameworks that manage to *restrict* information flow even more.

Signal Intelligence thrives in connections. Not formal cross-functional teams with governance structures. Just lightweight conversations between people who impact each other but rarely interact. Focus on pattern detection, problem identification, new thoughts vs. decision-making or governance.

Find two functions that affect each other but rarely talk. Or when they do talk, someone's crying in the bathroom afterward. You know the ones: Product and support playing their eternal game of "why didn't you tell us?" Sales and operations locked in their death match over what's possible. Marketing and customer success speaking entirely different languages about the same humans.

Hold brief monthly sessions (30 minutes, no more) where they share what they're noticing in their worlds that might matter to the other. Not to fix each other. Not to assign blame for past sins. Just: here's what's shifting in my world. Here's what I'm hearing. Here's what surprised me.

One company connected their sales and customer success teams for monthly 30-minute conversations. Sales shared the questions prospects were asking. Success shared the challenges new customers faced. Within two months, they'd identified a gap in their onboarding process that was creating churn six months post-sale. They fixed it before it showed up in quarterly metrics. Integration of perspectives instead of departments protecting their turf.

Monday: Identify two functions that impact each other but rarely connect. Invite representatives from each to a 30-minute conversation next week.

Next week: Hold the first session. Keep it informal. Ask: What are you noticing in your world that might affect the other team? What questions are you hearing? What's shifting?

Next month: Make it regular. Monthly works for most teams. Keep it light. Keep it conversational. Let insights emerge naturally.

These three practices work because they make space for what's already happening: people noticing patterns, sensing shifts, connecting dots. You're not building something from scratch. You're amplifying what already exists.

It's Already Here

A favorite movie line of mine is when Bill Paxton's Twister character growls, "It's already here!" about the tornado at the drive-in. Signal Intelligence often exists in your organization but isn't named, valued, or strategically leveraged. It hides as "experience" or gets dismissed as "overthinking" when it challenges consensus.

Remember the operations director from our opening story? She exists in your organization too; likely, several do. They're the people who sense shifts before others, raise uncomfortable questions, and see connections others miss. They're often labeled "difficult" in the moment, but "prescient" in retrospect. Your benched talent may be your best talent.

Here's how to spot them:

Look for the Early Warning Indicators

They sense issues before they manifest, often as mid-level managers or senior contributors who notice emerging patterns others miss. They might get eyerolls in meetings for raising concerns that later prove perceptive.

Listen for: "Something doesn't feel right about this rollout schedule." "I'm noticing a shift in how clients describe their challenges." "The team's energy changed after we implemented the new metrics."

Track Your Post-Crisis Reviews

When you review what happened after issues emerge, you'll often discover someone sensed the problem early but wasn't heard, or the organization wasn't ready to respond. Be prepared to find out that someone just flat-out dismissed it or blocked it. That's obstruction, not Guideship. It happens, and we can fix it.

Look for: Quiet concerns rationalized away, questions dismissed as "off topic," suggestions tabled for "later discussion" that never materialized.

Identify the Connectors

Signal Intelligence thrives in people who connect information across domains, asking seemingly unrelated questions that ultimately prove relevant.

Notice: People who bring perspectives from other departments, read broadly outside their field, and make unusual connections. Watch for team members who ask "what if" questions that seem tangential but reframe problems in illuminating ways.

Watch Decision Timing

Leaders with strong Signal Intelligence make decisions at the right moment. Not too early with insufficient information, but well before the critical tipping point.

Observe: Who shifts from exploration to decision at exactly the right moment? Who knows when to wait for more data versus moving forward? Who consistently gets the timing right, even without explicitly articulating how?

These people are assets. Trust them. Learn from them. Build systems that amplify what they already do naturally.

Who just came to mind as you read this? Because someone did. Could be you.

That person who sees patterns before others do. The one who raised concerns six months ago turned out to be exactly right. The team member labeled "not a culture fit" or "needs to be more strategic" or "overthinks everything."

Here's an uncomfortable truth: your process, your culture, your people operations might be the ones who benched them. Not maliciously. They were protecting the status quo, smoothing friction, managing perceptions. Someone raised questions that made leadership uncomfortable, so they got performance-managed into silence. Bypassed for promotion. Coached to "read the room better."

Go look at your last round of "culture fit" discussions. Your "not ready for leadership" assessments. Your "brilliant but..." feedback. I'd bet money you'll find your best sensors in that pile, labeled as problems instead of assets.

No? Were they **actual performance issues**? Then why are they still here? You committed to Guideship. Drift happens, people get scared, lose their way for a bit, become disoriented. Work with that. But Obstruction? Deliberate blocking? That gets zero oxygen in this culture.

If you're in leadership, this is your week to pull those people back in. Have the conversation. Acknowledge what happened. Ask what they're noticing now. Give them room to use what they see.

And if you're that person on the bench? Stop waiting for permission.

You Don't Need Permission

You don't need a leadership title to develop Signal Intelligence.

A mechanic at a car dealership noticed the same transmission issue showing up in a specific model right after the warranty expired. He started tracking it on his phone. During the weekly service huddle, he asked others about the trend. Two others nodded. He kept mentioning it. Eventually, his service manager escalated it. Manufacturing defect caught before it became a lawsuit.

He didn't wait for authority. He noticed, he tracked it simply, he asked if others were seeing it too. That independence, that willingness to trust what you're seeing even when nobody's asking you to look, that's how Signal Intelligence spreads.

You don't necessarily need the entire system to agree with you either. The best solutions sometimes start in the smallest places.

Start with your team. Your corner. Your function.

Add ten minutes to your next meeting to ask what surprised people this week. Track one early signal that matters to your work. Connect with one other team that impacts yours.

You can change how your immediate world operates without changing the entire company. Signal Intelligence spreads through practice, not policy. One conversation. One pattern noticed and named. One person trusting what they see enough to say it out loud.

You already sense things others miss. Now trust it enough to act on it. Your scope of influence is bigger than you think.

Getting Started, Creating Momentum

Here's the beautiful part... you don't need to transform anything.

No organizational redesign. No consultant-led initiative with a catchy acronym. No twelve-month roadmap with governance structures and success metrics. This allows natural systems to expand, come into equilibrium, and find their feral.

You just need to start noticing and talking about it.

Pick one thing. Monday works. Today works.

The next time someone mentions a pattern, no matter how slight, commit to stopping and asking questions right in the moment. When three different people mention the same friction point, recognize it's no coincidence, it's a clue. Track one thing that predicts what you care about instead of just measuring the outcome after it's already happened.

That's it. That's the revolution. Common sense + feral willingness, and you're executing.

The question was never whether you're capable of this. You are. You've been doing it your whole career, probably your whole life. The question is whether you trust yourself enough to act on it.

Signal Intelligence isn't elaborate. It's expanding your window of choice before you're forced into one. It's building capacity while you still have the luxury of time. It's creating foresight while "wait and see" still feels like an option.

That foresight?

That's hope in action. Real hope. The kind that creates options instead of just wishing for them.

You've developed Signal Intelligence, the capacity to read emerging patterns, make strategic decisions before pressure forces your hand, and solve problems while solutions are still simple.

Now we connect that intelligence to the systems that scale it: aligning purpose and vision across teams, embedding coherence into operations, and making strategy work in the real world where everything's messy and nothing goes

SIGNAL CHECK

SELF

What pattern have you spotted that others haven't connected yet, and what would it take to move from being right to being useful by acting on it now?

TEAM

As a team, where do we already see what's coming before it shows up in the dashboards, and how do we move from spotting problems to solving them while we still have options?

CULTURE

Looking across the organization, who are the people consistently spotting what's next, including ones we may have sidelined for asking uncomfortable questions, and what strategic advantage are we losing by not leveraging what they see?

CHAPTER SIX: THE COLLECTIVE STRATEGIC MIND

SEVEN

The Practice of Vision

GENERATIVE VISION FOR PURPOSE AND ALIGNMENT

The invitation arrived with full headquarters grav-i-ty! Subject Line: *Strategic Alignment Summit.*

The field managers came because you always come. By the first break, the a regional manager leaned over and muttered, "Seventeen new processes. Seventeen. From people who haven't touched a customer since the last ice age." You tried to hide the smirk in your coffee cup.

This is what misalignment feels like. Elegant rollouts that survive in planning but crumble in the real world. Field teams patching holes to serve real people while the center bristles at the improvisation. Everyone working hard, but not together.

I've lived in that middle. Translating executive vision into field practice and then dragging the field's wisdom back upstairs where it's often ignored. It wears you down. You end up as a bridge holding weight no one else acknowledges.

The fracture usually reveals itself through the people you serve. A client once told us, "We love working with you, but we never know which version of you we're going to get." That wasn't laziness or incompetence. It was a lack of coherence.

This is what happens when Signal and Vision live apart.

Strategy at the center. Reality in the field. Neither speaking the same language.

Signal shows what is happening, but without Vision to pull toward a shared future, it dissolves into firefighting. Vision without Signal becomes theater, admired but useless. Both are necessary. Neither is sufficient alone.

Generative Vision is different. It refuses to choose between clarity and adaptability. It creates coherence that holds difference without erasing it. It builds a compass everyone can carry, instead of a fragile map that only works in one terrain.

And this is where your stance matters.

A Guide uses Signal to see where drift is happening and Vision to expand what's possible. Guideship turns alignment into a practice of trust, not a compliance exercise.

Here's what that looks like in practice. Next time you're in a meeting where the plan looks perfect on paper, but you sense field resistance, try this: ask one quiet question. "What will this require from the people doing the work?" Not as a challenge. As genuine curiosity. That question opens space for Signal to surface before the plan calcifies.

Or when you're translating strategy downward, add one move: bring field wisdom back up with equal weight. Don't just report problems. Name what's working that headquarters can't see. That's how you stop being the bridge and start building the road both sides can walk.

Pause here. Where are you carrying too much weight as the translator? Where are you holding two sides of a system that refuse to meet? What would it look like if alignment wasn't your burden, but a shared practice of coherence?

This is the starting point. Not more rules. Not more slogans.

The work is to design the conditions where vision doesn't live in one office or one slide deck, but in the daily stance of everyone involved. When that happens, you don't just prevent drift. You create the possibility of movement that is both strategic and human, both ambitious and sustainable.

That's where Generative Vision begins. And you don't need permission to start. You need one conversation where you refuse to let Signal and Vision stay separated. One moment where you model coherence instead of waiting for someone else to mandate it. The people around you are already hungry for this. They're just waiting for someone to go first.

Signal Finds Problems. Vision Builds Futures

For a long time, I mistook being sharp-eyed for being effective. I could walk into a room and sense where things were breaking down before anyone admitted it out loud. That was my Signal work. Pattern recognition, drift detection, naming the cracks no one else wanted to see.

The problem was, I stopped there.

I thought diagnosis was enough. It isn't. You can be brilliant at spotting dysfunction and still have no influence, because people don't follow a list of problems. They follow direction that feels worth moving toward.

Here's what I missed: Signal tells you what's true right now. Vision shows you what you could build together.

Signal without Vision? You're standing in the rubble with a clipboard, cataloging damage. Vision without Signal? You're sketching castles while the foundation crumbles. Neither one works alone.

I learned this lesson the hard way. Back to my dysfunction-spotting superpower! I made immaculate recommendations that solved every visible issue. They were airtight, but they didn't land.

Why? Because I was offering fixes for what was broken when people were starved for something to build toward. They didn't need another map of potholes. They needed a compass that still worked when the road changed.

This is where the Seeds of Potential surface, often without announcement. Intention pushes Vision beyond clever slogans into a living choice: what are we here to make possible? **Inclusion** keeps Vision from narrowing into the same voices deciding the same outcomes. **Integration** pulls Signal and Vision together, so they don't operate on parallel tracks.

None of this comes from a workshop slogan.

It comes from choosing, daily, to build something generative instead of extractive.

If you're leading, the test isn't whether you can diagnose. It's whether you can generate futures that hold together under pressure. That's the Guideship stance. Turning raw data into coherence people can trust.

Try it this week. Next time you catch yourself cataloging what's broken in a meeting or a message, stop mid-sentence. Add one more line: "*Here's what we could build instead.*" Then sketch that future in plain language. Not a five-year plan. Just the next right thing that moves you closer to coherence.

Watch what happens when people have something to walk toward instead of away from.

Pause here. Where in your world are you stopping at diagnosis? Where are you pointing at what's broken and expecting others to feel inspired? What would shift if you treated every Signal you see as raw material for Vision, not just evidence of frustration?

The Curious know this already in their bones. You've spent time naming patterns, spotting drift, and identifying the story under the story. Now the practice is expanding Signal into Vision. The work is to imagine systems that don't just survive inspection but invite participation. The discipline is to speak with the confidence of a builder, not only the critique of a scout.

Generative Vision is how you stop being the person who is "always right but never followed." It's how you turn sharp perception into shared direction. That shift, from problem-spotting to future-building, is where your influence multiplies.

And it starts the moment you decide that every crack you name deserves a future you're willing to build.

Closing the Gap Between Values and Systems

Every person I meet tells me they hold values dear. Hang out with good people if that's not the same for you. They mean it, too, in the moment.

But every time I spot hypocrisy in myself, watch my own values get ignored in a tough moment, see myself rewarded for behavior I claim to reject, it's a step away from those values. Not toward cynicism. Toward extraction. And *what's true for us personally becomes systemic when we bring it to work.*

Many organizations have values written down somewhere. On the website, in the handbook, on glossy paper stuck to the wall. And every organization has the lived values; the ones people experience when decisions get made and power gets exercised. Professed or performed?

The gap between those two is where trust dies.

Take a look at a team talking endlessly about collaboration, only to find promotions handed out solely for individual wins. "Inclusive" leadership meetings where only certain voices ever shaped outcomes. The entire courage conversation that sits down quietly when hard truths arrive. So much for that arena.

That's not culture drift. That's gaslighting.

Saying one thing and rewarding another isn't a gap. It's a betrayal. The posters aren't the problem. They leave because the system makes a liar out of every guiding statement.

Here's the horizon: You can close the gap. The solution is elegant and simple. The systems must honor the claims. Simple and challenging. When compensation, recognition, and decision-making line up with stated values, trust regenerates faster than any speech can manage.

Let's talk about performance management and the favorite, 1 - 5 rating. It's hard for folks to hear 3, the solid "meets expectations," and not translate it to "average." It's even harder to watch leaders vacillate between 4 and 5 for the high performer. Is it exceeding or excellent? Is it exceptional or outstanding?

There's the jerk in the corner office that declares no one is perfect and never gives a 5, so the best anyone can get is an 80. Great, the lowest B possible. That's inspiring.

Steal my method. A 4 exceeds expectations and so does a 5. But a 5... they replicate. They're guides, every single time. They multiply excellence.

Someone exceeds but isn't generative? Can't (won't) bring others along? Never getting a 5. I've been pleasantly surprised at the clarity that comes. Collaboration and stewardship aren't nice-to-have. They are the path to advancement.

That shift offers more than clarity. It can reboot the culture. People begin to look for ways to lift each other, not just outshine each other. The system tells the truth, collaboration matters. When the system tells the truth, the values can be trusted.

Take pay equity. Many folks file it under belonging and inclusion, but it belongs here in Generative Vision. Lack of pay equity is an extractive practice. You can talk about fairness all day, but if two people doing the same work earn different salaries because of gender or race, the system is lying. And people know it.

Closing that gap isn't just right, it's how you prove the values aren't decoration. This is a place where reflection and action matter most. What will you change so the system tells the truth?

This is the work of Guideship. A Guide dismantles the hypocrisy and rewilds the structure so the professed values and the performed values match. It's messy. It often requires setting old processes on fire. But it's the only way forward.

Take a moment and look at your own environment, workplace, team, even family. Where is the gap between what's said and what's rewarded? Where are you still letting someone treat values like suggestions? And what system could you change, big or small, that would make the value real?

The Curious know this: values are covenants. They are promises you make and keep together. And once people believe the promise is real, they'll give you energy, creativity, and commitment that no incentive program can buy.

When Signal names the hypocrisy and Vision insists on coherence, systems begin to align. That's when purpose regenerates trust instead of draining it.

The Infrastructure Everyone Ignores

Here's what most vision work misses. The real work is aligning systems. And systems have more influence on daily decisions than any inspirational speech ever will.

I was leading a team through a major transition. I had perfect clarity about what needed to change. I could articulate the vision with evangelical fervor. I had buy-in from leadership and enthusiasm from the team.

Six months later, we were right back where we started. People cared. I'd tried to change behavior without changing the infrastructure that shaped behavior.

The meeting structures rewarded whoever talked loudest and longest. The performance review process measured individual achievement while collective impact got a participation trophy. The project approval system made maintaining the status quo easier than trying anything that might move the needle.

You know what's heartbreaking? I've facilitated leadership development programs in company after company, industry after industry. Most of them are outstanding cohorts with strong cultures supporting them.

Sometimes, though, I watch guides get genuinely excited about new processes and approaches. They're energized. They're ready. They see exactly how these tools could transform their teams.

Then comes the moment of truth. They look at each other and admit: "This is brilliant, but it can't survive back home."

Do as I say, not as I do became the unofficial motto everywhere I went.

These leaders know what good looks like. They've experienced it. But they also know their organizations will punish them for trying to implement it. So they go back to environments that systematically kill everything they just learned, carrying tools they can't use and insights they can't act on.

Let's be clear about what's happening here. This isn't about weak commitment or lack of courage. It's about power. Systems protect themselves. Sometimes with the best of intentions and the biggest smiles. If you don't have positional authority to redesign those systems, trying to act against them can cost you credibility, advancement, even your job. That's not paranoia. That's pattern recognition.

What do you do when you can see the infrastructure hindering good work, but you can't destroy it?

You start smaller. You work at the edges where you have control. Change the meeting structure for your team, even if you can't change it company-wide. Reward collaboration in the ways you can influence, peer recognition, project assignments, how you talk about wins. Make one process easier to navigate. Create one pocket where experimentation doesn't require three layers of approval.

The breakthrough came when I stopped trying to overcome bad systems with good intentions. Instead of begging for different behavior, I redesigned the environment that produced behavior. Instead of pleading for collaboration, I restructured incentives to reward collective outcomes. Instead of hoping for innovation, I made experimentation easier than compliance.

People didn't have to fight their systems to live the vision. The systems made living the vision the deliberate choice.

Where are you carrying tools, you can't use because the infrastructure won't allow it? What's one system within your sphere of influence, however small, that you could redesign this month? Not the whole organization. Just your corner of it. What would shift if you stopped waiting for permission to make the infrastructure match the vision?

You don't need total control to create pockets of coherence. You need Signal to see where the systems betray the stated values, Vision to imagine what could work better, and Guideship to build it at the scale you can touch. Those pockets spread. People notice when something works. And they start replicating it in their corners too.

Vision Lives in Your Stance, Not Your Title

Most people wait for authority before they practice vision. They imagine influence comes with a title, a budget, or a corner office. But Generative Vision doesn't require position. It requires stance.

Think about the woman working in a healthcare system obsessed with throughput metrics. Patient flow ruled every discussion. Efficiency was worshipped. Actual patient care was something that got mentioned in mission statements but ignored in daily operations.

She had zero authority to change organizational priorities. But she had something more powerful than permission: she practiced Vision in every conversation.

In meetings dominated by numbers, she asked, "How might this affect the patient experience?" Not as a weapon, but as a lens. When presenting her team's results, she didn't stop at the metrics. She added, "Here's how this scheduling change reduced stress for families." She wasn't critiquing. She was modeling a new standard.

Over time, her colleagues began asking the same questions. The stance spread.

That's how Vision works when it's generative. You don't declare it. You embody it until others can't imagine working any other way.

Signal sharpens your awareness. What's breaking down, where people feel disconnected. Vision stretches those insights into a future worth moving toward. Guideship makes it portable. You don't need a title to stand in coherence, to connect today's work to tomorrow's meaning.

This is true professionally and personally. The way you operate at home, in community spaces, in conversations that feel small, it all matters. People are always watching. Not to judge, but to see if what you say matches what you do.

When you practice Generative Vision in one space, it reshapes how you show up everywhere. And others notice. They feel the difference. They start asking themselves if they could operate that way too.

Where are you waiting for permission to lead with vision? Where are you quiet because you don't hold the microphone?

What if you started smaller, asking one better question in a meeting, reframing one result in terms of human impact, weaving one thread of purpose into the daily language of your team?

The Curious know this truth: leadership without authority isn't theoretical. It's contagious. You don't need to command vision. You live it, and others will carry it forward. That's how trust multiplies. That's how coherence spreads. That's how the future gets built in places still waiting for permission.

When Clarity Becomes a Cage

Clarity feels good at first. Everyone exhales because they finally agree on a direction. The words sound sharp, the numbers look clean, and the room feels steady again.

The problem comes when that clarity hardens into a cage. You've seen it happen. A team finds a breakthrough and locks it down. What worked becomes what must always work. The plan looks flawless, and no one wants to be the first to ask if it still makes sense.

This is what happens when clarity loses its flexibility.

> ### Clarity slides into comfort, comfort into complacency, complacency into rigidity.

Marketing keeps recycling a campaign that no longer lands. Operations perfect efficiency until there's no space left for imagination. Leaders confuse decisiveness with progress.

The pursuit of excellence becomes perfectionism. And perfectionism drains energy, kills creativity, and makes people afraid to try.

Generative Vision handles clarity differently. It treats vision like a compass that keeps you oriented but leaves space to move. Signal helps you notice the warning signs: energy flattening out, quality used as an excuse for delay, teams hesitating because the plan feels untouchable. Guideship reopens the door to curiosity. Excellence comes from learning and iteration, not flawless execution.

Think of a leader who sets high standards but still praises an early draft. That simple move makes experimentation safe. Or a team that stops mid-project to ask what they've learned that might change direction, not just whether they're "on track."

Where has your own clarity drifted into rigidity? Where have you mistaken delay for quality? What would shift if you defined excellence by what was created and made useful, not by how perfect it looked?

Thriving never comes from flawless performance. It comes from staying alive to possibility. Generative Vision keeps clarity from turning brittle. It gives people permission to build, test, and grow without fear of being wrong.

Now picture a team that treats curiosity as fuel, not a threat. Where excellence grows from bold tries, not from waiting until every angle is polished. That is clarity at its strongest. Steady enough to give direction, flexible enough to let people thrive.

What Spreads Beyond Your Reach

The work you do doesn't end when the meeting closes or the project wraps. Every act of Guideship seeds expectations that people carry with them into the next room, the next role, the next organization.

That's the quiet power of Generative Vision. It travels.

Think about the last time you worked under someone who made coherence real. Not just talk, but systems that matched the words. The memory of that doesn't fade. You remember how it felt to be trusted, to have your ideas taken seriously, to see purpose show up in the small decisions.

Once you've tasted that alignment, you cannot unknow it. You start looking for it everywhere else.

Signal plays its part here. It helps you notice not just the cracks but the sparks, the places where belonging and meaning are alive. Vision stretches those sparks into something bigger, showing people what is possible when energy regenerates instead of drains. Guideship makes the stance portable. When you lead with coherence, others carry that stance forward even when you're gone.

I once watched a young manager learn what real inclusion felt like. Decisions in her team didn't stop with the usual suspects. Everyone had a seat and a say. She carried that memory into her next job, and the next.

Now she builds it in everywhere she goes. It wasn't in her handbook. Someone gave her a living example of how it works.

That is the ripple effect of Guideship. Guides create more guides.

What do you want people to carry out of your space? Not another list of commitments. A lived memory that says, "This is what trust feels like. This is what purpose tastes like. This is how it feels to thrive."

Those experiences become the standards that others refuse to lower again.

You do not need a global platform to shape the future. You need daily stances. The commitments we walked through earlier. What do I choose? Is my behavior aligned? Do I have the capacity? Do I have the knowledge?

One conversation where you connect results to human impact. One system that rewards collaboration instead of competition. One moment where you refuse to let curiosity be punished.

Those choices ripple farther than you will ever see.

The Curious already know this. You want your work to matter beyond the spreadsheet, beyond the quarterly cycle. You want the people you guide to leave with more than skills. You want them to leave with a felt sense of coherence, trust, and courage that they will recreate in places you will never step foot in.

That is how Generative Vision outlives you. It spreads not by mandate but by memory, carried forward by those who experienced it.

Your legacy lives in the people who walk into their next room unwilling to accept less than what they've already built with you.

SIGNAL CHECK

SELF

Where are you stopping at diagnosis instead of building futures, and what would shift if you treated every problem you spot as raw material for what you could create next?

TEAM

As a team, where is the gap between our stated values and what actually gets rewarded, and what's one system we could redesign this month to close that gap and rebuild, or strengthen, trust?

CULTURE

Looking at where strategy meets execution across the organization, is any infrastructure quietly undermining the vision we claim to hold, and what would become possible if we redesigned systems to make living our values the obvious choice?

CHAPTER SEVEN: THE PRACTICE OF VISION

EIGHT

The Navigation Problem

RELATIONAL GRAVITY FOR TRUST AND BELONGING

The line cook has stopped moving.

It's 5:47 PM on a Friday, thirteen minutes before the dining room opens, and the kitchen should be humming. Prep stations dialed in, tickets staged, everyone in rhythm. But the line cook is standing at his station, staring at his mise like it's written in a language he used to know.

The chef notices. Fresh from binge-watching a Bourdain marathon and convinced rage is a management strategy, he starts yelling.

The line cook doesn't flinch. *He just... stands there.*

He's not lazy. He's not checked out. He's disoriented.

I'm convinced that most of what we're calling disengagement is disorientation.

Disorientation isn't the same as disengagement. When you're lost in the wilderness whether you've lost the trail, separated from the group, or your GPS died, the first step is to STOP. It makes you easier to find.

The line cook has stopped because he doesn't know which direction is forward anymore, and survival instinct says: stay put, stay calm, wait for someone to come get you.

We miss this clue and start labeling. Quiet quitting. Checked out. Low morale. Burnout. We roll out surveys and employee appreciation days and hope the energy comes back. We blame the very people who are waiting for us.

He's waiting to be found, *and he won't wait forever.*

If no one comes, if the system keeps shifting and no one acknowledges he's lost, he'll stop waiting. He'll walk off the line, out the door, into the next job that at least pretends to care.

This isn't a morale problem. It's a navigation problem. And it's happening everywhere.

Relational Gravity is what orients people when everything else is shifting. It's trust. Trust that doesn't need a crisis to prove itself. Trust that your contributions matter. Trust that someone will notice when you're lost. Trust that the relationships around you are real enough to survive honesty.

The question isn't whether your people are engaged. It's whether you're coming to find them. Or whether they've already figured out you're not.

We can stop here for a second and check for orientation, or disorientation.

- Where are you mistaking disorientation for disengagement?
- Where have your people stopped moving, not because they don't care, but because they're waiting for someone to notice they're lost?
- And how long do you think they'll wait before they stop waiting?

Relational Gravity isn't built in a retreat or a workshop. It's built in the daily practice of noticing when someone has gone still and choosing to move toward them instead of past them.

The line cook is still standing at his station. Doors open in eleven minutes. The question is whether anyone's paying attention.

Trust Isn't Neutral

You're in the meeting where the project management tool gets rolled out. Again. This one's different, they promise. Better integrations.

Clearer workflows. Real-time updates that will finally solve the communication problem.

Except it won't. Because the communication problem isn't about tools.

You can have forty-seven different apps tracking what three people used to remember. Crystal-clear protocols. Organizational charts that make consultants weep with joy.

But when trust breaks down, everything breaks down. And **trust breaks down fastest for people who already have reasons to question whether they truly belong**.

Slack channels buzz with activity but deliver zero real communication. Daily standups happen but transparency doesn't. Collaboration tools hum along while collaborative spirit stays absent. The infrastructure of productivity is running. The infrastructure of relationship is dead.

The infrastructure of belonging? *Never even built.*

This is where Inclusion stops being a nice idea and becomes structural. It's not enough to hire people from different backgrounds if you don't build systems that help those differences become strengths instead of sources of quiet isolation. Metrics are easier than culture. Diversity numbers look good on paper.

But without relational practices that account for who feels held and valued, you're just collecting people.

Trust and relationships share a common bond. They don't stay neutral. They're either getting stronger or weaker with every single interaction.

For people who face systemic barriers to belonging, that math is even more complex. *Every interaction carries the weight of history, identity, and the constant calculation of safety.*

Teams where trust compounds make every challenge easier to handle together. Teams where trust degrades unevenly force some people to work harder to prove themselves while others move through the space with ease.

The difference isn't luck or chemistry or "culture fit" (that phrase meaning "people who remind us of ourselves"...please, stop using it). It's **Intention**. The choice to build Relational Gravity that accounts for the reality that not everyone starts from the same place of assumed belonging.

You can create psychological safety without bubble-wrapping challenge and risk. But first you have to notice where the infrastructure is missing entirely.

- Where are your tools humming while your people stay disconnected?
- Where have you built systems for productivity but not for relationship?
- This week, choose one place to build infrastructure that supports people, rather than tracking them.
- The tools won't save you. The relationships might.

Where Attention Goes, Trust Follows

You're at The-Table-Everyone-Wants-A-Seat-At when it happens. The room is loud, everyone contributing. The loudest voices all share similar backgrounds. The women are talking, yet their ideas keep getting talked over or mysteriously attributed to someone else ten minutes later. The two Black engineers are participating, but they're spending twice as much energy proving their points as everyone else.

Then Maria raises a concern about a feature that could alienate Latina users. The room goes quiet. Someone dismisses it as "too narrow" and "not data-driven enough."

Maria stops speaking for today, and maybe always.

In that moment, you've created a masterclass in selective hearing.

Your focus on collaboration and "healthy conflict" (corporate speak for "let's argue without anyone getting fired") forgot to account for power dynamics.

Who got to speak without interruption. Whose ideas got built upon versus dismissed. Who could disagree without being labeled "difficult" or "too emotional" or whatever code word makes dismissal sound professional.

Attention is a resource. Where you direct it shapes who gets to build trust with you. Trust becomes conditional the moment only certain voices get amplified, only certain perspectives get prioritized, only certain people get the benefit of the doubt.

This is where Intuition matters. You sensed the shift before anyone said it out loud. The energy changed. The pattern revealed itself. Now you have a choice about what to do with that Signal.

Inclusion isn't a workshop. It's a daily practice of noticing where your attention flows and choosing to redirect it toward the voices you've been missing. It's recognizing that some people have to work twice as hard to be heard once. Integration means redesigning the conditions so that stops being true.

You don't need a new system. You need one move that proves you're paying attention.

- Next meeting, ask Maria directly what she thinks before the room gets loud.

- When someone gets talked over, stop the conversation and bring them back in.

- When an idea gets mysteriously reassigned, name it out loud: "I think that was Maria's point from earlier."

- When someone's contribution gets dismissed as "not data-driven," ask what data would be convincing, and whether you're holding everyone to the same standard.

These aren't big gestures. They're *redirections of attention*. And they're how trust starts becoming equally accessible instead of conditionally available.

Where is your attention flowing by default? What would it cost you to redirect it this week toward one voice that's been waiting?

Relational Gravity means relationships strong enough to hold everyone, not just the people who already remind you of yourself.

That's how trust stops being conditional. That's how **Inclusion becomes structural** instead of performative. That's how people stop calculating whether they belong and start building what matters.

When Star Teams Collapse

Jake's manufacturing team stops you in your tracks. For two years, they've been untouchable. Cross-trained, collaborative, crushing every safety and productivity target thrown at them.

Then the plant gets acquired.

New ownership. New metrics. Tighter deadlines. Constant surveillance from corporate types who've never worked a line in their lives.

The pressure is intense, but they've handled pressure before. What they haven't handled is how that pressure reveals fault lines nobody noticed when things were smooth.

The supervisor starts micromanaging instead of trusting people to move. Independence evaporates. Team members who used to cover for each other start tracking who's pulling their weight like they're running a workplace audit. The informal mentoring disappears as everyone focuses on individual survival. Integration, the very thing that made them great, falls apart.

Within six months, they go from star performers to highest turnover and most safety incidents. No one forgot how to do their job. They lost the *relational foundation* that made their technical skills effective.

We obsess over fixing low-performing teams while high performers implode in silence. We ignore high performers on autopilot while begging low performers to just...could you just be...mediocre? All our coaching, feedback, and energy goes toward dragging them to average. Maybe.

Meanwhile, the resignation from the high performer comes at 10pm.

We assume. The metrics are good, so we're good. They look happy, so they are happy. I haven't heard anything, so nothing's wrong. By the time we notice the cracks, half the team is gone, and HR is wondering about the turnover spike.

Relational Gravity strong enough to hold smooth conditions isn't automatically strong enough to survive turbulence. Pressure either makes teams tighter or exposes every weakness. The difference is whether you've built trust that can handle weight.

Where are your high performers showing strain? What would it cost you to check in before they collapse instead of after?

You don't need to wait for the implosion. Trust that spidey sense of **Intuition** whispering that something is going on and it's time to talk to people. Ask the questions that make you uncomfortable.

Stop Smoothing What You Should Be Solving

One of your team members is undermining another. Not loudly. Championship-level passive-aggressive behaviors on display. Subtle dismissals in meetings, credit taken for collaborative work, and tasks that mysteriously don't get coordinated. You've noticed it for weeks. You keep hoping it'll resolve itself.

It won't.

You're smoothing over (*procrastinating, postponing, abdicating, ignoring*) what you should be solving. And the person being undermined? They're calculating whether it's safer to stay quiet or start looking for the exit. Meanwhile, someone is looking at **you** wondering when you became so conflict avoidant.

When you finally address it directly, you realize you're months late and a dangerous cascade is in play. The undermined employee has already started disengaging. The one doing the undermining is shocked you're bringing it up because you never said anything before. And the rest of your team has lost respect for your ability to lead.

Intuition told you something was off weeks ago. You saw the pattern. You felt the shift. But you didn't act because you weren't sure how, or you hoped the problem would fade, or you didn't want to make things awkward.

Meanwhile, trust eroded every single day you stayed quiet.

Relational Gravity isn't built through big interventions or cringe-worthy conversations about feelings. *Pro-Tip: Stop doing therapy at work. It's unethical, you're not qualified, and everyone's uncomfortable.* It's built when you address what's happening instead of pretending everything's fine.

Next time you catch yourself smoothing over tension instead of solving it, stop. Name it directly. "I've noticed you dismiss Maria's contributions in meetings. That stops now. Here's what I expect instead." Clear. Direct. Done.

Psychological safety doesn't mean protecting people from discomfort. It means trusting that **bad behavior won't be tolerated** and **good work won't be invisible.**

Teams get stronger under pressure when people know you'll address what's broken instead of pretending everyone can't see it.

When Team Cohesion Becomes the Barrier

We don't always recognize how our vision of "good" can close the door to progress. Strong team cohesion can become a barrier to new people. The very relationships that make a team effective can also make it impossible for anyone else to break in.

Picture a team that's been together for three years. They've developed an almost telepathic ability to collaborate. They finish each other's sentences, anticipate needs, and solve problems with minimal conversation. It's beautiful.

Then they hire two new people who bring different approaches and different communication styles.

The existing team isn't trying to exclude anyone. They're just efficient in ways that are impossible for newcomers to navigate. Inside jokes, shorthand references, unspoken agreements about how workflows. The new hires are technically capable, but they can't crack the social code.

Within six months, both transfer to other teams. Not because they couldn't do the work, but because they never felt like full members despite producing results.

This is the dark side of Relational Gravity: the stronger the bonds, the higher the wall. When someone asks, "Why do we do it this way?" the answer is usually "Because that's how we do it." Forget about being **Inquisitive**, questions are for the experienced. **Improvisation** dies. The team stops adapting because they've perfected a system that only works for the people who built it.

The solution isn't to weaken existing relationships. It's to be **Intentional** about extending trust to new members. *Make the implicit explicit.* Treat every "dumb question" from a newcomer as useful Signal about what you've stopped examining.

Strong teams don't just protect what they've built. They expand it to hold more people without losing what makes them strong.

What Spreads Without Permission

When you get Relational Gravity right, something remarkable happens. It improves your direct relationships, of course, you expected that. Did you realize it would influence how people relate to each other, even when you're not around?

Jennifer had been working on building stronger relationships with her customer service team. More consistent feedback. More thoughtful about how decisions landed on different people. More intentional about creating space for contributions that usually got talked over.

The shift didn't happen in her one-on-ones. It happened between team members when she wasn't in the room.

They started checking in with each other without being asked. Addressing conflicts directly instead of letting them fester. The woman who'd been the only Spanish speaker on the team stopped being the go-to for "difficult calls" and started getting asked for input on how to communicate better with everyone.

Jennifer didn't train them to do any of this. She just modeled what it looked like to treat relationships as seriously as results. And people started replicating it.

This is how Relational Gravity spreads: not through policies or team-building exercises or trust falls (please, stop with the trust falls). It spreads through lived experience.

When people feel what it's like to be in relationship with someone who takes their full humanity seriously, they start creating that for others. For some of them, you'll be the first. And that changes everything.

> ## You don't mandate trust.
> ## You model it. Be trustworthy.

And then you get out of the way and let it multiply.

The Ripples You May Never See

This work extends far beyond your current team or organization. Every person who experiences strong, inclusive Relational Gravity carries that expectation forward into their next role, their next team, their next organization.

They become leaders who understand that relationship health isn't separate from performance excellence but foundational to it. They seek out and create work environments where people can bring their full selves without fear of judgment or exclusion.

They refuse to accept toxic team dynamics as "just how business works."

The impact compounds. Organizations that consistently hire people who've experienced real Relational Gravity start operating differently. They develop cultures where trust doesn't have to be built from scratch with every new project because the underlying systems support connection rather than undermine it.

The ripple effects extend into communities, families, and other organizations as people bring these relational skills to every part of their lives. They become the people who know how to build connection across difference, who can maintain relationships under pressure, who understand that human flourishing and collective success aren't competing priorities.

What you're practicing requires **Intention.** The choice to model trust instead of demanding it. We can stop asking about teaching others to trust more. Ask instead how each of us can become more trustworthy.

Think about one person on your team or in your orbit. What are you modeling for them right now? Is it something you want them to carry forward into their next role, their next team, their next leadership position? If not, what needs to shift?

Where are you the first example? Where are you showing someone what trust looks like in practice, not just theory? And what would it mean if they carried that standard into every room they enter for the rest of their career?

Your legacy isn't the systems you built. It's the people who walk into their next role unwilling to accept less than what they experienced with you.

The Long Game You're Playing

What you're practicing isn't just management or leadership development. It's a form of social change that happens one relationship at a time, one team at a time, one organization at a time.

In a world that seems increasingly fragmented, where people retreat into like-minded groups and trust across difference feels rare, you're proving that another way is possible. Teams can be both high-performing and genuinely inclusive.

Organizations can honor both *individual excellence* and *collective care*. Success doesn't require sacrificing humanity.

This isn't naive optimism. It's practical intelligence applied to the reality that human beings do their best work when they feel genuinely connected to the people around them. When they trust that their contributions matter. When they know they won't be abandoned when things get difficult.

The research backs this up, even if your organization hasn't caught on yet. Teams with strong Relational Gravity outperform fragmented ones on every metric that matters. Retention. Innovation. Speed of execution. Ability to navigate ambiguity. The capacity to take smart risks instead of playing it safe.

But you're not doing this just for the outcomes. There's more.

Work consumes a third of most people's waking lives. Spending that time in environments that erode trust, punish vulnerability, and reward performance theater is soul-crushing.

The exhaustion comes not from hard work but from constantly calculating whether it's safe to be honest. The loneliness of showing up in spaces where no one sees you.

You're building the alternative. Not because it's trendy or because some consultant sold your CEO on psychological safety as a competitive advantage.

You refuse to be complicit in systems that treat people as expendable.

You refuse to be complicit in systems that treat people as expendable.

That refusal is Intention in action. And it's contagious.

The organizations that figure this out will have an enormous advantage. They'll attract talent that others can't. They'll keep people who would otherwise burn out or walk. Complexity that shatters more fragmented teams becomes navigable.

Innovation that requires deep trust, the kind that survives disagreement, failure, and pressure? That becomes possible too.

Most importantly, they'll be sustainable. Not in the buzzword sense, but in the human sense. They'll be powered by energy that regenerates through connection instead of depleting through competition. They'll be places where people can do their best work without destroying themselves in the process.

This is Relational Gravity at full strength. Not just holding teams together when things get tough but creating the conditions where everyone's best contribution becomes possible. Where people stop performing engagement and start building something that matters.

- Where are you refusing to be complicit?
- What system are you quietly redesigning so it stops extracting and starts sustaining?
- And who's watching you do it, learning that refusal is possible?
- You've now moved through **Signal Intelligence**, learning to notice what most people miss. **Generative Vision**, learning to build futures worth moving toward instead of just diagnosing what's broken. And **Relational Gravity**, learning to create trust that doesn't evaporate when stakes rise.

But trust is the floor, not the ceiling.

You can have perfect Signal, compelling Vision, and rock-solid Relational Gravity, and still watch everything stagnate. Because seeing clearly, knowing where you're going, and trusting the people around you doesn't automatically create movement. It creates readiness.

What comes next is the part that makes most leaders uncomfortable: **Creative Instigation**. I know! It needed to be bolder than innovation, more challenging than think-outside-the-box.

We're so jaded, we need to remember the thrill of sparking something new. Of disrupting what's long petrified. Of building solutions that didn't exist before you showed up. Of moving from diagnosing problems to solving them in ways that create change and serve visions.

The world has plenty of people who can spot dysfunction, place blame, and prescribe remediation. What it desperately needs are people who can do all that in human and visionary ways *and then make something happen.*

Not through force or authority. Through creative provocation that shifts what's possible.

Let's go there now!

SIGNAL CHECK

SELF

Are you mistaking <u>disorientation</u> for <u>disengagement</u> in the people around you, and what would shift if you stopped waiting for them to ask for help and instead moved toward them first?

TEAM

As a team, where have we built infrastructure for productivity but not for relationship, and what's one practice we could start this week that proves we notice when someone has gone quiet?

CULTURE

Looking across the organization, where is trust breaking down unevenly, forcing some people to work twice as hard to prove themselves while others move through with ease, and what would it take to build Relational Gravity that holds everyone, not just those who already fit?

CHAPTER EIGHT: THE NAVIGATION PROBLEM

NINE

The Spark of Momentum

Courage and Creative Instigation

The meeting has been going forty minutes, and no one's said anything useful.

Forty minutes of smart people staring at a problem that matters. Real stakes. Real consequences. Everyone's gone still, not thinking, bracing.

Someone finally breaks the silence. "What if we just do what we did last time?"

Everyone nods. Relief disguised as agreement.

And the meeting dies right there.

This is what happens when systems confuse agreement with progress.

Somewhere along the way, you learned that being creative is dangerous. I've often felt like I must choose between being smart **or** creative, instead of being smart **and** creative.

You've been told to be innovative. Encouraged to "think outside the box." Asked to be creative, whatever that means, if you don't make anyone uncomfortable.

But here's the truth: innovation doesn't start with creativity.

Innovation starts with instigation.

Innovation improves. Inspiration uplifts. Influence persuades. Instigation moves.

It's the force that turns a room full of thinkers into a team of doers. It's what gets people to leap, to pivot, to act in counterintuitive ways. It's what makes someone say yes to the hard thing, the wild thing, the necessary thing. Climbing Everest. Jumping out of airplanes. Changing careers. Reporting the danger. Naming the name.

And that takes talent. Not the kind you list on résumés. The kind that can read human resistance and redirect it in real time.

Good instigators don't push people off cliffs. They invite them to jump into courage. (Well, beware the bungee-jumping types. They think it's funny.) They sense exactly when fear is disguising itself as logic. They know how to move people toward what matters, even when it defies comfort, precedent, or data.

Instigation isn't chaos. It's **catalytic design.** It's knowing when to apply friction, when to apply fire, and when to back away so others can step forward.

And yes, it's dangerous. Systems addicted to safety will always label movement as threat.

That's why people like you get called *difficult*. You ask for action where others want more meetings. You say the real thing when others are still "aligning language." You're the one who starts the motion everyone later calls momentum.

And yet, they'll say they want creativity. They'll say they want innovation. What they want is **instigation without the discomfort.**

But movement has a cost. Something must shift. Someone has to go first.

And that's you.

Creative Instigation is the courage to start what needs starting. Not to be loud or rebellious, but to make aliveness contagious.

It's the refusal to wait for permission to act on what's already clear.

It's the spark that says: *we can't stay here.*

That's what you've been learning all along, how to move systems, not just ideas. How to ignite possibility, not perform compliance. How to spark change that sticks because it's rooted in something real.

Instigation isn't rebellion for rebellion's sake. It's the practice of motion in a world that rewards stillness.

So go ahead. Be the one who starts the fire everyone pretends to want.

That's what a creative instigator does.

Why Smart People Go Silent

If you've ever watched a room of brilliant people go quiet, you know it's not because they have nothing to say. It's because they've been trained to wait.

We've spent decades teaching humans to obey. To follow the rubric. To color inside the lines and please the graders. We call it school, performance reviews, best practice, alignment. Then we're somehow shocked when they don't leap at the chance to try something new.

Inventive thinking isn't magic. It's a muscle. And like any muscle, it weakens when you stop using it.

Organizations have spent years training you **not** to be creative. Approval processes that punish experimentation. Metrics that reward efficiency over exploration. Cultures that celebrate compliance over curiosity.

We talk about innovation, but we promote obedience. Domestication of the feral becomes the goal.

Brainstorming sessions become painfully awkward performances that sound like first dates between people who already know they're incompatible. Lists of ideas filed and forgotten because no one expects anything to happen. It's why "brainstorming" ranks right up there with "role play" for least-loved work activities. The awkward. So. Much. Awkward.

And it starts early.

Third grade: You raised your hand with an answer that was close but not quite right. The teacher corrected you in front of everyone. Laughter. **Lesson learned:** *stay quiet unless you're sure.*

First job: You suggested a new approach. Your boss said, "We've already tried that." Everyone nodded, even though it wasn't true. **Lesson learned:** *don't challenge what's already been blessed.*

Last month: You floated an idea. Someone immediately listed three reasons why it wouldn't work. No one asked how it **could. Lesson learned:** *imperfect equals wrong.*

By the time you're leading teams, you've internalized a lie so deeply you don't even notice it anymore: creativity is for creative people. And you're not one of them.

Except that's garbage.

You solve problems creatively every single day. You reroute your commute when construction blocks your way. You renegotiate timelines when life intervenes. You talk a teammate off a ledge and still deliver the work.

That's invention. That's improvisation. That's guideship in motion.

The problem isn't capacity. It's captivity.

Systems that praise obedience can't produce innovation. They can only replicate what's already known. You've been trained to protect what exists instead of creating what's next.

That's why the room goes quiet. Not because people don't care, but because they've learned that caring out loud is dangerous.

Here's what blocks creativity inside teams:

- **Fear of looking stupid.** Ideas that aren't fully formed get treated like confessions of incompetence. So, people wait until they're 100% sure, which means they never speak up, because certainty is a myth. If you only reward fully baked ideas, you'll never taste anything fresh.

- **Reverence for precedent.** "We've always done it this way" isn't analysis. It's surrender. But it's safer than suggesting something untested, so precedent wins.
- **Confusing critique with intelligence.** The fastest way to sound smart in a meeting is to explain why something won't work. Tear down ideas. Cite risk. Reference past failures. Congratulations, you sound credible, and you've killed momentum. The person who builds gets called naïve. The person who destroys gets called strategic.

That's what we've built entire organizations around; risk aversion dressed up as rigor.

Let's fix it with a fundamental reframe of what creativity is and how it works.

Creativity isn't magic. It isn't decoration. And it isn't reserved for people with design degrees or artistic temperaments.

Creativity is a practiced response to constraint.

And constraint? You've got plenty of that.

Building Under Pressure

Remember that project where you had all the time and money you needed? The one that somehow produced the safest, most forgettable outcome imaginable? Projects with unlimited time and budget rarely make history.

But the one where half your resources vanished, your best person quit, and the deadline got pulled up two weeks? That's the one people still talk about. The one that somehow worked.

The difference wasn't genius. It was pressure that demanded focus.

Constraints aren't punishment. They're permission to stop pretending you can do everything. They strip distraction down to signal. They make you name what matters. Some of us eat that like candy.

You've lived it. Give a feral leader a tight deadline and the impossible becomes oddly efficient. Give them endless time and they'll alphabetize their snack drawer. I know because I do it. When time stretches wide, I start curating playlists instead of producing paragraphs. But when a date looms? Fire. Procrastinators, you know this dance.

The blank page paralyzes. The constrained canvas liberates.

Dr. Seuss wrote *Green Eggs and Ham* using only fifty words because his editor bet him he couldn't. The limit didn't cage him. It focused him into one of the best-selling children's books of all time.

Improvisation works the same way. Jazz musicians don't panic when handed four bars in C minor. They don't beg for more room. They play inside the form until the air catches fire. The form isn't confinement. It's ignition.

Your job isn't to dodge constraints. It's to collaborate with them. Treat them as design partners, not death sentences. When the budget shrinks or the timeline collapses, stop asking how to work around it. Ask what it's trying to teach you.

A cut clarifies. A limit reveals. **The right question changes everything.**

When your training budget got slashed, you couldn't send everyone to a three-day conference anymore. So, you built your own one-hour peer sessions where staff taught each other what they knew best. Cost almost nothing. Engagement skyrocketed.

The constraint wasn't the problem. The assumption was.

Now, let's talk about perfection. The obsession with getting it right before anyone sees it kills more good ideas than bad leadership ever could. Teams polish slides until they sparkle, then discover they solved the wrong problem. Leaders wait for complete data and end up deciding too late.

Perfectionism is the respectable face of fear. We've rewarded it for decades, then wondered why creativity flatlined. It's time to release the fantasy that everything and everyone must perform at 100 percent all the time.

Improvisation shifts that completely. More than "yes, and" kind from workshops. The one that says: build it rough, test it fast, learn what breaks, fix it, repeat.

A marketing team with six weeks to launch didn't have time for perfect. They had time for prototype. They tested a messy first version with ten customers in the hallway. Feedback was brutal. They rebuilt. Three days later came version two. Still flawed, still improving. By launch day they'd tested seven versions. The final one worked because they learned by doing, not polishing.

That's **Inventive** thinking in motion. Not waiting for the perfect idea, building your way to it.

Try this: take something you've been perfecting and test it incomplete. Don't wait until it's pretty. Share it rough. Ask three people, "What's confusing here?" Then rebuild from what you learn.

The goal isn't to launch garbage. It's to learn faster than your competitors can plan.

Constraints don't block creativity. They refine it. They turn flailing effort into precision.

And that's where breakthrough lives.

What Becomes Possible

The compliance team dropped the new regulation on your desk like a death sentence. Every product communication now needed sign-off from three departments: Legal, Medical Affairs, Regulatory. Average approval time? Six weeks.

Your competitor immediately pulled their entire direct-to-consumer strategy. Too slow. Too expensive. Too risky. The industry consensus was clear: this regulation had just killed patient engagement.

Your team spent two days in mourning. Then someone asked the wrong question.

"What if this isn't a restriction? What if it's pointing us toward something better?"

Everyone looked at her like she'd lost her mind.

But you didn't shut it down. You looked her straight in the eye. "Keep going."

"We've been trying to tell patients what to do. What if we helped them tell **us** what they need? We don't need approval to listen. We only need approval to speak."

Three weeks later, your team built something no one in the industry had tried. A platform where patients shared their experiences, asked each other questions, and surfaced the patterns that mattered most to them. You didn't create the content. You created the conditions for others to create it.

The regulation that was supposed to silence you made you better listeners. The constraint that killed your competitor's strategy gave you access to insights they'd never have the courage, or humility, to hear.

Six months later, patient retention had doubled. Not because you talked more. Because you finally shut up and learned.

Your competitor is still waiting for their old playbook to be approved.

That's **Creative Instigation.** Not working around the constraint. Not optimizing despite it. Using it to invent what couldn't have existed without it.

The limitation didn't just focus your creativity. It revealed an entirely different game.

Making Creativity Collective

Here's the truth nobody wants to hear: your individual creative brilliance doesn't scale.

You can be the most *Inventive* person in the room, but if your team waits for your next idea like it's a weather report, you haven't built creative capacity. You've built dependency. It's happening more than you realize.

Innovation isn't a solo sport. It's a team discipline. The difference between teams that create and teams that execute is whether problem-solving is shared or bottlenecked through a few people.

You've seen the bottleneck version. The team that goes quiet when the "creative person" isn't there. The group that waits for leadership to fix things instead of tackling them together. The organization where innovation dies the moment the founding genius leaves.

That's not innovation. That's a single point of failure with a fancy title.

Integration is what makes creativity collective. It's not a mindset poster or a retreat theme. It's how a team thinks, works, and learns. And it starts by changing the conditions that make creativity optional.

If your team's only "creative" moment happens during a scheduled brainstorm, you've already lost. Those sessions reward performance, not experimentation. Everyone shows up to prove they're clever instead of getting curious.

You've been in that room. Someone says, "Let's brainstorm!" with the forced enthusiasm of someone who's never done it before. Everyone gathers around the whiteboard. The problem gets written neatly at the top. Then silence.

A safe idea. Some polite nods. Another slightly safer idea. More nods. The loudest person in the room takes over while everyone else starts mentally checking email.

This isn't creativity. It's performance art.

Research backs it up. Individuals working alone generate more ideas than groups brainstorming together. Why? Because group dynamics reward conformity and caution. While one person talks, the others wait. Waiting kills momentum. Add hierarchy to that mix, senior people dominate, junior folks self-edit, and the best ideas stay unsaid.

I assure you; the ideas are there. Your team has more creativity than you'll ever need. Currently, it's in a vault that an Oceans movie would struggle to open. You can do this.

If you want real creativity, build the conditions for it.

Start small. When your team hits a problem, resist the urge to solve it yourself. Ask, *"What could we try?"* not *"What should we do?"* The first invites experimentation. The second demands certainty nobody has.

When someone presents a constraint, don't accept it as final. Ask, *"How might this limitation point us toward something better?"* Make that your default question, not a novelty.

And redesign your brainstorms. Call them something else while you're at it.

Give everyone five minutes of silent idea generation before anyone speaks. No discussion, no groupthink—just ideas. Then share them anonymously. You're evaluating ideas, not people.

Once the conversation starts, the **only rule is simple: *build, don't debate.*** "Add to it", "What could make that wilder?", "What can we layer it with?", "Keep going."

If you need structure, use constraints. Instead of "How do we improve customer service?" try "How do we improve customer service using only what we already have?" Limitations focus energy. They don't restrict it; they refine it.

And please, **stop rewarding the person who finds the flaw faster than the path forward**. Critique disguised as intelligence is the fastest way to kill momentum. And if you do it, you don't sound smart when you shut things down. You sound scared.

Want to make creative thinking collective? Measure it. Track how many ideas were tested this month. How many assumptions were challenged. How many times someone said, "Let's try it," instead of, "Let's check." What gets measured gets valued, and what gets valued gets repeated.

Diversity matters here more than anywhere else. Homogeneous teams converge on the same safe answers. Diverse teams collide, irritate, stretch, and create. The irritation is part of the ignition. **Inclusion isn't a checkbox. It's your raw material.**

Try this this week. Pick one problem your team is facing. Before discussing solutions, have everyone write down three possible approaches, the weirder, the better. You're not after the right answer. You're building the **Inquisitive** muscle. Then prototype the most promising one. Don't perfect it. Just test.

Watch what happens when people witness creativity being welcomed right in front of them. They see it with their own eyes, proof it's real. The wonder of catching Santa Claus mid-delivery.

The energy changes. Quiet people find their footing. Cynics get curious again. The team that used to freeze starts moving because creativity isn't a special event anymore, it's the way work gets done.

That's the goal. To make Inventive, Improvisational thinking part of the ecosystem, not a feature of the few.

Creativity that depends on one person burns out. Creativity that belongs to everyone builds systems strong enough to outlast you.

And when that happens, when a team becomes fluent in building, testing, reframing, and inviting difference, innovation stops being a miracle. It becomes muscle memory.

Demonstrating collective intelligence that doesn't freeze under pressure. It flows.

Building Systems That Multiply Invention

You've watched teams create breakthroughs under pressure. You've also watched them snap back to safe, predictable thinking the moment the pressure lifts.

The difference isn't talent or motivation. It's whether creativity is built into how work happens or treated like a special occasion someone has to schedule.

Most organizations treat innovation like an off-site hobby. They bring in consultants, run workshops, even open an "innovation lab" far from where the real work lives. Then they wonder why nothing changes.

You're building something different. Systems that make creative problem-solving the default, not the exception.

Start with decision points. In every team meeting, ask, *"What are we assuming that might not be true?"* Not as a gimmick, but as a forcing function. Last month your team debated how to speed up a report. Then someone asked, *"What if we're reporting the wrong things?"* Turns out half the data hadn't been used in years. The solution wasn't faster. It was smarter.

Build in experiment budgets. Not for brainstorm theater. For real tests. You've carved out ten percent of project time for ideas that might not work. If something can be tested in two weeks with existing resources, it doesn't need approval, it needs curiosity and a clear way to measure what happens.

That's Improvisation made systematic. Seventeen tests last quarter. Eleven failed. Six worked well enough to keep. That's a better innovation rate than most R&D departments can claim.

Reflection loops. After every project, a fifteen-minute harvest: *What did we learn that we didn't expect?* Not a post-mortem. A learning extraction. You're capturing **Intuition**, the pattern recognition that emerges when people are in the work instead of observing it from a distance.

When budget cuts hit, you don't shrink. You reframe. *"What if this constraint is pointing us toward a better solution?"* That's **Inventive** thinking as reflex, not rescue.

Make creative capacity visible. Track it. Celebrate it. How many experiments this month? How many assumptions challenged? What constraints became opportunities?

What gets measured gets valued. And what gets valued gets repeated.

That's how you build Integration at scale. Not relying on a few moments of brilliance but multiplying the Inventive mindset across the entire system.

The Muscle You're Building

Remember that meeting? The one where everyone went silent because suggesting something new felt too risky?

Here's what happens when you rebuild the muscle.

Someone names the constraint. The budget's cut. The timeline's compressed. The client wants something that doesn't exist yet.

And instead of freezing, someone asks, "*What becomes possible because of this limitation?*" Not despite. **Because of.**

The room doesn't go quiet. It gets curious. People start building on each other's ideas instead of defending their own. Someone suggests testing a rough version by Friday. Someone else volunteers to prototype it. A third person spots a connection no one else saw.

This isn't magic. It's practice.

You've been building something across these four channels, and it's starting to compound.

Signal Intelligence taught you to notice what others miss. To read patterns, sense shifts, and trust your Intuition before the data confirms it.

Generative Vision gave you a North Star worth moving toward. Not just diagnosing what's broken but shaping futures that don't exist yet. Making purpose visible enough that others can see it too.

Relational Gravity built the steady trust when stakes rise. Relationships strong enough for people to take risks together. To be honest when things aren't working. To extend trust across difference, not just toward those who already agree.

And now **Creative Instigation.** The capacity to spark something new. To turn constraints into fuel. To prototype your way to breakthrough instead of perfecting your way to irrelevance.

Individually, each of these capacities matters. Together, they transform how you move through the world.

You notice what's shifting... **Signal**. You name where it could lead... **Vision**. You build the trust that makes bold moves possible... **Relational Gravity**. You create solutions that didn't exist before you showed up... **Creative Instigation**. Do you see how powerful your **Guideship** is, and needed in this world?

This is the Confluence, the power of rivers of information and practice coming together.

When you combine pattern recognition with purpose, trust with invention, intuition with action, you stop reacting to what's happening. You start shaping what happens next.

The frozen meeting doesn't happen anymore. Not because your team got more creative, but because you built systems where creativity is the default, not the exception.

Constraints don't paralyze. Problems don't linger. Your team treats them as invitations.

You've built integrated capacity. Compounding power.

And this doesn't stop with you. Everyone who experiences what's possible when someone leads with Signal, Vision, Gravity, and Instigation carries that expectation forward.

That combined power, of strategy, vision, trust, and innovation, is what moves us into *The Delta*.

Where the river meets the ocean. Where what you've built becomes something far larger than you.

You're ready.

SIGNAL CHECK

SELF

Where have you been waiting for the perfect idea or the right moment, and what would it take to test something rough this week, learn from what breaks, and build your way forward?

TEAM

As a team, where are we treating constraints as problems to solve instead of design partners that could reveal better solutions, and what becomes possible if we ask "because of" instead of "despite"?

CULTURE

Looking at how innovation happens across the organization, have we built systems that reward safe repetition over bold experimentation, and what would shift if we measured creative capacity as rigorously as we measure efficiency?

CHAPTER NINE: THE SPARK OF MOMENTUM

The Delta
Influence Flows Outward

EXPANSION

TEN

The Gravity of Wholeness

THE LIVING SYSTEM OF INFLUENCE AND IMPACT

Feel that shift when you step into a challenge now, when you speak up, when you walk with that quiet, **earned** confidence?

Not the old masks. Not the rehearsed calm or the half-smile of performance anxiety that hides what you think. **Something else.** Something that *lands* instead of flinching.

When the hell did that happen?

You know that moment when someone points out the **mycelial network** under the forest floor and suddenly you can't unsee it? Miles of living thread connecting everything that looked separate. Roots passing warnings, sharing strength, keeping the whole forest alive. And you think, *Wait! This has been here the whole time?*

That's your leadership right now.

Go ahead, look around. *Seriously.* What you've been building isn't a set of skills you deploy like gadgets from a leadership Swiss-Army knife deployable on demand. It's one living system, expanding under everything you touch.

You might be wondering, *Did I build all that?*

Yeah. You did. And here's the wild part: it's working even when you're not thinking about it. When you stop trying to prove integration and start **being** integrated.

You've moved beyond leading differently. **You are different now.** At home, at work, with partners, colleagues, cultures. You're creating the **Guideship DNA** that will outlast you.

When It All Clicks (And You Stop Trying So Hard)

Picture that last crisis. Yesterday. Last week. There's always one sitting firmly in recent memory. Camped there, talking to us.

The client bailed. Three departments launched a blame parade. Your boss went full meltdown, demanding answers you didn't have and fixes nobody could conjure out of thin air.

And you? You exhaled. Not a technique, not a trick. Just that deep, cellular knowing that rises when your body remembers, *Oh right. I know how to lead through fire.*

Everyone else scattered into their favorite crisis costumes — Captain Spreadsheet, Drama McDeflector, Miss "I Sent an Email," and the PowerPoint Hero, valiantly formatting slides while Rome burned. You stayed present. You asked the question nobody wanted to touch: *Where are we guessing?*

The room went still. You could feel the collective gulp, the sudden quiet when performance runs out of script. Then, finally, the real conversation began.

That's not integration happening. That's **you, integrated.** No checklist. No pep talk. Just clarity doing what clarity does.

Stop calling it luck. Stop wondering if you imagined it.

You've crossed the line between building capacity and *wielding it*.

The question isn't whether you can handle complexity anymore. It's the legacy you'll build now that you can.

When you stay grounded while the system loses its mind, gravity shifts. People start orbiting toward you. You're not trying to hold them together. **Steady things pull chaos into coherence.** Physics.

Notice how they respond. The woman from finance now brings you the problems she used to bury in spreadsheets. You don't have *Finance* in your title. You listen for what's real instead of what's rehearsed.

Your team doesn't fidget through meetings anymore. They finish each other's sentences. They hand you half-formed ideas because they know you'll treat curiosity like currency, not risk.

You didn't train them to do that. Didn't send them to a workshop called "How to Trust Your Leader More." You modeled it. You stayed whole long enough for them to remember what it feels like to work with someone who is present and guiding.

And now? Now you're dangerous.

People who can stay steady while everything burns don't fix problems. They rewrite the **conditions** that created the problems. They ask the question that makes everyone else think, *Damn. We've been solving the wrong thing this whole time.*

What are you going to do with that power? And more importantly, who's watching you learn how to use it?

The Effect You Never Saw Coming

There's a moment you realize you've been teaching people things you never meant to teach.

Your nephew starts negotiating with his friends using your exact style, the pause for effect, the calm redirect, and you think, *When did I become the influence here?*

Or your boss drops your favorite phrase, the one about *making space for what's emerging*, in a board presentation like it's theirs. Word for word. With that confident nod you know they practiced in the mirror.

That's what happens when your Signal aligns.

People leave your meetings feeling different. Like they just remembered they have spines. They start asking better questions in other meetings. They stop tolerating the organizational shenanigans that used to pass for leadership.

That energy? It spreads.

I know a department head who couldn't figure out why people kept showing up to her team meetings uninvited.

First, it was one person from marketing, sneaking in quietly. Then someone from operations, pretending they had a "quick question." Within weeks, half of engineering was there too, notebooks open, looking sheepish but absolutely refusing to leave.

Finally, she asked, "What the hell is going on?"

One of them shrugged and said, "We *heard you have real conversations here.*"

That was it. No fanfare. Just word spreading about a place where people could tell the truth.

In her meetings, problems that once took three committees, two consultants, and a prayer circle to fix were solved in twenty minutes. People left energized instead of exhausted. Departments that hadn't collaborated since flip phones were cutting-edge suddenly started working together. People left energized instead of wondering if they could fake their own death to avoid the next quarterly review.

No executive launched a culture initiative. People had tasted what it felt like to be real. Once you've tasted that, you can't go back. I'm firmly convinced this is behind the rise of solopreneurism. People tasted it, couldn't find it again, and crafted their own.

That's what your presence is doing. Creating permission.

You thought I was kidding when I said, "Guides create more guides."

People watch you navigate chaos without losing your center and think, *Wait. Maybe... I don't have to choose between being effective and being human. Maybe... I don't have to cosplay competence while my soul slowly dies.*

You're not teaching them techniques. You're showing them what wholeness looks like in motion. And it's spreading fast, through people who are tired of performing sanity in systems that reward fragmentation.

Once someone experiences what it's like to work with a leader who's whole, they can't unsee it. They start noticing the careful word choices, the strategic emotions, the polished nothingness that passes for professionalism.

You've ruined them for mediocre leadership. And honestly? Good.

The effects are already rippling farther than you can see. The only real question now is: **Are you ready for what happens when everyone expects this level of realness?**

Building Bridges You Didn't Know Existed

You're operating between worlds now, and it's getting weird in the best possible way.

The startup accelerator where every sentence ends with *scale fast*. The nonprofit coalition where passion runs high but the annual budget couldn't buy a used Prius. The corporate boardroom where everything is measured, benchmarked, and emotionally unavailable.

Different planets. Different gravity.

And here you are, the one who can breathe in all of them.

Somewhere along the way, the code-switching stopped. No more corporate mask for executives, authenticity costume for nonprofits, or hustle face for founders trying to prove they still sleep. That exhausting wardrobe is in storage now.

You just show up. Same you. Same presence that reads the room like a weather system. Same capacity to ask the question everyone's avoiding because, honestly, *someone must*.

Last month you sat in a merger discussion where two companies couldn't even agree on the color of money. Cultures miles apart. Values alphabetized but never lived. The consultants had been tap-dancing for weeks.

You asked one question: *What are both sides most afraid of losing?*

Twenty minutes later they were designing solutions together.

You didn't drop a framework or flex your résumé. You brought the same grounded presence that works when you're translating TikTok metrics for a board of silver-haired investors *and* when you're talking budget triage with your twenty-something idealists.

You've become a universal translator. People see you walk into the room and think, *Oh good, the one who makes sense is here.*

And they're right.

You're not speaking different languages anymore, you're listening beneath them.

That's what integration feels like in motion. The ability to move through wildly different ecosystems without splitting yourself into acceptable versions.

It's not shape-shifting. It's coherence.

You stopped needing to perform belonging, and now you just *belong*.

That's the real bridgework.

The Culture Shift Nobody Planned

You know how organizations spend millions on "culture change" that flatlines by Q3?

They bring in consultants who look like they ironed their personalities. Share workbooks, wallet cards, and swag with words like *Integrity* and *Innovation* in fonts that cost more than a used car. Host all-hands meetings where executives read from scripts about "embracing change" while their body language screams, *Please don't change anything important, or difficult, or really, well, anything.*

Most fail because they're decorating the walls instead of changing how it feels to work there.

Your integration is doing something entirely different. You're changing the *experience*. One real conversation at a time.

When you create space for pattern-sensing in that remote team call, the twenty-two-year-old developer stops pretending she understands everything and starts asking what matters. When you ground that budget meeting in purpose, the CFO remembers why they ever wanted this job. When you address tension head-on, people stop wasting half their energy on underground politics.

Those shifts don't stay contained in a neat little box labeled *Team Development.*

The developer carries her courage into her next role. The CFO starts asking better questions in other meetings. Your department stops tiptoeing around the elephants that have been squatting in every room for years.

Culture doesn't change because someone sends a memo about it. It changes the moment people experience something real and think, *Wait. We could work like this!*

That's what you're creating. Presence as practice. Wholeness as default. Integration as the way things get done.

And it's spreading faster than anyone expected. Through departments, across industries, through generations tired of pretending.

One brave, honest response at a time.

When The Old Ways Push Back (And They Always Do)

Oh, they're coming for you now.

"You're being too philosophical."
"We need someone more results oriented."
"Can we get back to business fundamentals?"
"This feels very… touchy-feely."

Translation: *Please go back to fragmenting yourself so we can feel comfortable again.*

This is the test. The moment when the system tries to convince you that your wholeness is the problem. That asking real questions "slows things down." That caring about people somehow competes with getting results, as if humans aren't the ones doing the work.

Here's what I need you to remember when they bring their carefully constructed cages:

You're the one who stayed calm when everyone else lost their minds during the last crisis. *You're the one* who saw the solution nobody else could see because you weren't too busy managing your image to think clearly. *You're the one* whose team still wants to do their best work instead of surviving until Friday.

They're not mad about your results. They're mad about your method.

Integrated leaders are harder to control. You ask questions that reveal inconvenient truths. You notice patterns everyone else pretends aren't there. You create space for conversations that challenge the lies whole systems are built around.

That's exactly why the world needs you to stay whole.

Don't you dare apologize for bringing your full self...anywhere. Don't you change to make others comfortable. Don't shrink back into the polite version of yourself to keep the peace.

Presence outpaces permission every single time.

Let them be uncomfortable. Let the old systems creak under the weight of your wholeness. That sound? That's progress.

Teaching Without Trying

You're teaching without realizing it. You are a walking masterclass in possibility and hope.

Every meeting you run differently plants seeds. Every decision you ground in purpose shows people what alignment looks like. Every relationship you tend with care proves that business and humanity aren't enemies after all.

Remember, integration is the mycelial network, connecting, thriving, and moving resources where they're needed most. Knowledge is a resource. Authenticity is a resource. Agency and choice are resources.

You're not trying to convert anyone. You're being yourself. And that's revolutionary.

That marketing director who now starts campaign reviews by asking what outcome they're trying to create? She watched you do that once in a budget meeting and thought, *Oh. We can ask that question.*

The operations manager who finally addressed the tension between the two team leads instead of pretending it would fade on its own? Your influence, spreading and evolving.

You're modeling what it looks like when someone refuses to split themselves into acceptable pieces.

And people are hungry for that. Starving for it.

The systems around you are malnourished from performative leadership and allergic to truth. When someone like you shows up, present, whole, unedited, the ecosystem wakes up. It's the magnificence of watching natural ecosystems emerge, restored, after a dam is removed on a river.

Teaching that doesn't announce itself. That changes what people believe is possible by being in the same room.

The Long Game You Didn't Know You Were Playing

While everyone else optimizes for quarterly numbers, you've been building something that outlasts job descriptions.

That twenty-six-year-old engineer who can sense patterns before systems explode is carrying that skill into her next three companies. The collaborative approach you pioneered between feuding departments will outlive you too. Other organizations will study it when they realize it worked through presence, not process.

This is culture design the next generation will inherit. One where people don't have to choose between effectiveness and humanity. One where integration isn't a luxury you add after success, but the very thing that makes success possible.

This is generational work. You're not waiting for permission to do it. You're shaping legacy through behavior, not branding. Through conversation, not campaigns. Through choices that restore trust instead of eroding it.

Ready to own the fact that people are making career decisions based on what they learned while working with you? Because they are.

And someday, when you're not in the room, someone will quote you without even realizing it. A phrase. A question. A story you told in passing. It will shift a meeting, steady a decision, or remind someone of what wholeness feels like.

That's the long game. You don't control it. You don't even see most of it. You keep showing up whole and let the ecosystem do what ecosystems do.

You've been playing for legacy this entire time. You didn't know it yet.

How Far the Signal Travels

Notice how your influence keeps stretching beyond what you ever planned? You set out to fix a team problem and ended up rewilding culture. You wanted better decision-making and discovered you were changing how entire systems behave.

Your integration scales because it doesn't depend on tricks or titles. The same presence that transforms a one-on-one conversation reshapes a board meeting. The same pattern sensing that steadies your local team helps you navigate industry-wide tension.

Think of the delta where a river meets a larger body of water and expands into something vast. It carries everything it has learned downstream into new territory. That's you now.

A living confluence of everything that has worked, now flowing into systems hungry for leaders who can handle nuance without losing themselves.

Those systems are responding. They are looking for stability that does not require control. They are listening for signals that sound like courage and coherence.

You are the signal. You are the steady current moving under the noise.

Your reach is no longer a matter of scope or title. It is measured in resonance, in the way your steadiness travels through others and alters how they choose to lead.

This is how far the signal travels. This is what happens when guides stay whole. Their work keeps moving long after they leave the room.

Finding Your Folks

You know how to spot them now, don't you? The ones who choose wholeness over performance.

They're the nonprofit director getting competing organizations to work together. The startup founder building culture while scaling fast. The government official finding creative solutions in bureaucratic swamps. The consultant who changes clients just by showing up differently.

You recognize them by how they handle complexity. By how they stay present during conflict. By how they ask questions that matter instead of questions that sound smart.

These are your people.

As your signal strengthens, you start finding each other everywhere. Not through networking or strategy decks, but through resonance. You don't need matching titles or industries. You just know when you've met one of your own.

There's a shorthand between you. A way of listening that cuts through the noise. A sense that you can skip the pleasantries and start right where it's real.

When you connect, everything accelerates. The ideas, the collaborations, the courage. It's not competition anymore. It's ecology.

You were never meant to do this work alone. The systems you're influencing are too big, too complex, too important for any one person to carry.

But together, you're creating a network that doesn't need approval to exist. A living system that grows through trust, curiosity, and motion.

You're not trying to change the world. You're demonstrating what happens when people refuse to fragment themselves for other people's comfort.

Turns out, that's exactly how worlds change.

The Depth of Integration

Here's something I want you to understand, integration isn't a finish line. It's a practice that keeps unfolding. Every new challenge reveals another layer of bringing your whole self to the work. Every expansion of influence calls for a deeper level of trust in your own capacity.

You'll never be done with it. And that's the point.

The moment you think you've got it figured out, life will hand you a situation that asks for muscles you forgot you had. A conflict that tests your compassion. A change that shakes your certainty. A system that needs more patience than you thought you possessed.

Good. That's exactly how it should be.

Integration happens while you're moving. People talk about integration like it's some special moment. One day...you'll wake up fully integrated and never have to think about it again? Like there's some mystical moment when you get your "Wholeness Certificate" and can finally relax? Wishful. Thinking.

Every messy challenge becomes material for deepening your practice. Every new horizon becomes a mirror that shows you how far you've come. Every moment when the old, fragmented version of you would have split into acceptable pieces, you choose to stay whole instead.

Here's what I love about where you are now: you've stopped trying to perfect this and started trusting it to evolve with you.

And the results are everywhere.

Look around. The meetings where people finally speak the truth. The decisions that honor both humanity and reality. The cultures that are shifting one real conversation at a time.

You're not *using* integration. You're *proving* it works.

Across generations. Across industries. Across all the spaces where leadership still forgets that people are not performance tools.

You're building a future where wholeness is normal. Where complexity isn't feared but navigated. Where leaders stop performing and start belonging to the systems they shape.

You're not too much. You're right on time.

The mycelium is spreading. The roots are deepening. The forest is remembering how to thrive.

And you? You're no longer a single tree. You're a part of the network that feeds everything else.

Welcome to your influence. Guide from your wholeness like the future depends on it.

Because it does.

SIGNAL CHECK

SELF

What are you building right now that will outlast your current role, and where is it showing up in places you didn't plant it?

TEAM

Who in your orbit is becoming a guide because they watched you stay whole under pressure, and what shifts when you realize modeling is the mentoring?

CULTURE

What would you burn down tomorrow if you knew the guides in your organization were strong enough to rebuild something better from the ashes?

CHAPTER TEN: THE GRAVITY OF WHOLENESS

ELEVEN

The Return to Center

THE RESONANCE OF FERAL GUIDESHIP

The first person to feel your shift is *you*. It sneaks up in the quiet moments. You catch yourself breathing instead of bracing. You notice that voice in your head getting softer. The one that used to narrate everything you said or did with a running critique. Now it just... listens.

Your Signal, the way you show up, the energy behind your words, the stance you hold, is being **perceived, received, and believed** in *the way you intended*. You can feel it.

A colleague notices it first. The way you no longer frantically check email between meetings. How you listen to conflict instead of mentally drafting your response. Others bring the messy problems they used to hide. You won't make them feel foolish for not having it figured out.

Your team senses it too. Same agenda. Same conference room. But when someone says "everything's fine" while their project is clearly imploding, you don't let it slide. Not with judgment, but with curiosity. *What would help?* becomes your default response instead of "Let me know if you need anything."

You can ask yourself, "What would help me now?" without guilt, stories, or grief.

Even the colleague who used to dominate every discussion finds himself pausing to hear what you think. You haven't become louder. Something in your stillness commands attention. You ask the question that cuts straight to what everyone else is dancing around. The room shifts when you speak because people know you're not going to waste their time with diplomatic noise.

You're not trying to be anything anymore. *You're being everything you are*, and everyone feels it. Including you.

What You No Longer Tolerate

Clarity feels different now. It isn't sharp or defensive. It's clean. You know what belongs in your world and what doesn't, and you don't apologize for tending that line.

You've stopped mistaking *tolerance* for compassion. You've learned the cost of giving endless benefit of the doubt, it erodes focus, fractures energy, and feeds doubt. You don't need that lesson again. There may be hard conversations to have after spending time with me here in these chapters.

Now you can feel distraction in your body. The meeting that drifts without purpose, the colleague whose chaos hunts for company, the urgency that arrives without impact, all of it lands as noise, and you simply choose not to absorb it.

And when you need a loving reminder from me?

- The meetings that exist only to schedule other meetings. *You don't show up to them anymore.* When pressed, you suggest they send you the decision via email and ask if there's anything specific they need from you. Most of the time, *there isn't*.

- The colleague who turns every conversation into a competition about who's busier. *You stop playing along.* When they launch into their latest crisis, you listen for exactly thirty seconds, then redirect: "Sounds intense. What do you need?" If the answer is just an audience for their drama, you find somewhere else to be.

- The expectation that you'll be available for every "urgent" request that isn't urgent at all. *You've learned to ask, "What happens if we handle this tomorrow?"* Usually, nothing happens. The world keeps spinning. Projects continue. People solve their own problems when they realize you're not going to solve them *instead*.

- You don't announce your boundaries. *You live them.* When you find yourself slipping into the old, domesticated ways, the nice one, the people pleasing one, the conflict avoidant one, you pause instead of performing.

- When impostor thoughts come calling, whispering in the voices of ghosts of bosses past, beliefs past, generational trauma, all the old ways...*you don't debate them.* You recognize them for what they are: outdated programming that doesn't fit the current version of you.

> **This isn't detachment.
> It's devotion.**

Every clear no is a way of protecting your yes.

You're choosing value over comfort. You're not guarding against others; you're guarding your purpose. For every soul that ever said to pay attention to your priorities, you're now crystal clear on them. Don't be surprised when the same person, or system, is angry when they realize priorities don't place them first.

You refuse to collude with urgency addiction. You pay attention to what matters.

Boundaries aren't about keeping people out. They're how you keep yourself in. In purpose. In integrity. In alignment. In your center.

What You Can Trust Now

You can finally trust yourself.

No, not that curated one. Not the second-guessing one, over-explaining one, came-with-the-receipts and 97 back-up plans one. The real one, the you who knows when something feels right, and when it doesn't.

Remember, feral.

Feral is the **rewilded posture of leadership** that treats resilience and feedback as assets, honors lived experience as knowledge and embodies originality rather than imitation. A state of self-awareness and trust where a person **moves with confidence in their experience and expertise.**

It is the stance of a leader who claims **contribution and success without apology**, acknowledges mistakes with faith in their ability to recover and grow, and resists the grip of impostor syndrome, perfectionism, and self-doubt.

You've stopped cramming yourself into leadership boxes and started trusting your full constellation of capacities.

You can trust what your body tells you before your mind catches up. The flicker of hesitation in a conversation. The lightness when something aligns. The weight that lands when you're off purpose. You used to call it **intuition** like it was separate from logic. Now you know better. It's all one system, reading signal before data can translate it.

Intuition isn't some mystical power reserved for people who burn sage and read tarot cards. It's pattern recognition running faster than your spreadsheet brain can keep up. Your subconscious catching signals your conscious mind hasn't catalogued yet. Strategic intelligence that doesn't need a consultant's validation to be **right**.

You've learned the difference between intuition and anxiety. Anxiety makes you rigid, pushes you toward safe choices, insists you need more data before you can move. Intuition makes you *curious*, points you toward what needs exploring, trusts you can course-correct as you learn.

You can trust your rhythm. When to move. When to wait. When to speak truth even when the room wants comfort. You don't need a playbook for timing anymore. You have presence.

When the "perfect" solution keeps getting delayed for reasons no one can articulate, you pay attention to the hesitation instead of pushing through it.

You can trust your independence. You don't contort yourself to fit hierarchies or personalities. You bring your full capacity to the table and let it speak for itself. Collaboration is no longer a coping mechanism. It's *a conscious choice, a creative act.*

You can trust your inquisitive and exploratory nature. The questions you ask aren't detours from productivity. They're the pulse of discovery itself. The moment you start to sense something new taking shape.

You can trust your integration. The pieces you once treated as separate, logic and intuition, structure and creativity, leadership and self, have learned how to breathe together. Ecotones producing more variety, more options, more solutions.

Your Signal is clear now because you've learned to trust the full range of who you are.

You can trust that you are the guide now. You always were.

The difference is you finally believe it.

The Questions That Used to Haunt You

They still whisper sometimes, but they don't run the show. You hear them, smile, and keep walking.

Am I doing this right? There isn't one right way. There's your way, shaped by experience, refined by feedback, anchored in intention. That's what makes it trustworthy.

What will they think? They're thinking about themselves most of the time. The ones worth listening to will see you more clearly now. You're no longer hiding behind effort.

Am I too much? You're exactly enough for the work that calls to you. The right people don't flinch at your range; they rely on it.

Do I belong here? You belong anywhere you choose to show up as yourself. Belonging isn't permission. It's presence. It's something you **claim**.

What if I'm wrong? Then you'll learn, adjust, and keep going. Being wrong while being real is infinitely better than being right while performing.

You used to ask those questions from fear. These questions don't torture you anymore because you've found the answers in your own experience. Not in theory, but in practice. Not in your head, but in your *life*. Now you have space for new ones, from curiosity, from trust, from center.

What am I learning? What's possible here? What wants to emerge through me next?

That's the shift. You stopped auditioning for certainty and started collaborating with growth.

The haunting has ended. Only resonance remains.

How You Move Through Familiar Spaces

The rooms are the same, but you are not.

You prepare the way you always have, but there's no over-preparing now. No rehearsed lines. No contingency plan for every objection. You walk in knowing what you think, and *why* you think it.

When someone challenges your perspective, you don't shrink or trot out some appropriate response while real creativity dies in your mouth. You listen, steady and unthreatened, then respond with clarity instead of choreography. The calm that once took effort, or wasn't within your range, now arrives on its own.

You tell the truth kindly but without spin. You give context without apology. When they ask for the polished projection, you offer reality. When they look for the story that flatters their comfort, you hold up the mirror that reflects their growth.

The strange thing is, they respect it more than they ever respected your perfection. Turns out people are hungry for truth delivered with grace, for confidence that doesn't need a spotlight.

Your presence is the new power in the room. It draws people toward what's real. It changes the pace, the tone, the air itself. You've traded performance for presence, and the result is unmistakable authority, assured, unwavering, whole.

You move through familiar spaces easily now because you finally trust the one moving through them.

Your People and Your Work

It's funny how both found you once you stopped chasing either.

You no longer network for opportunity. You *resonate* into alignment. The people and work that belong with you recognize the frequency you're carrying now, steadiness, clarity, curiosity, trust.

The junior colleagues seek you out. Not for promotion or praise, but for guidance they can feel will be real. They know you'll tell them the truth about whether their idea has legs, whether they're ready for the next level, whether what they're chasing still matters.

The clients arrive earlier in the process now, before the mess turns into a crisis. They trust your read of risk because you don't soften truth to make them feel better. They know that when you say it will work, they know you believe it will.

Projects move faster. There's less noise, less posturing, fewer detours into performance. Decisions hold because they're made from clarity instead of compromise. You're not managing personalities anymore. You're managing purpose.

Your Signal is clean. **What you mean and what you say are the same thing.** Yes, you'll miss sometimes, but now you know how to come right back. And the right people feel it instantly.

But "your people" aren't only at work. They're the ones who remind you that wholeness was never meant to stay inside a meeting room. They're the ones who meet you where you're real, the friend who asks nothing but honesty, the partner who matches your peace, the family you build through choice as much as chance.

You're finding that when your life and your leadership share the same values, everything starts to work better. The conversations. The projects. The mornings. The relationships. The rest.

The work that finds you now feeds you instead of draining you. It stretches your imagination without collapsing your boundaries. You contribute at full strength without performing a version of yourself to fit in.

You've become magnetic to what's meant for you and invisible to what isn't.

You don't need to audition anymore. You already belong to the work and to the life that matches it.

Coming Home to Feral

This is what resonance feels like. The frequency of your outer world finally matching the rhythm inside you. No more adjusting your volume to be heard. No more smoothing your tone to make it palatable. No more proving what's already true.

Just you. *Full signal. Unedited. At home in your own skin.*

You can feel it in your nervous system, the way your breath comes easier now. The way quiet feels full instead of empty. The way you walk into a room and don't shrink or scan for cues. You belong because you decided to.

This is why the work used to feel so hard. You were trying to be capable in ways that were never yours. You can't force a river to run uphill.

Now you're moving in your natural direction. With your grain instead of against it. Using your strength instead of apologizing for it. Leading with rhythm instead of resistance.

You've come home to yourself. *To the version of you* that trusts what you sense. *To the guide* who knows when to rest, when to rise, and when to reach for help. *To the human* who can love and lead without splitting in two.

You've returned to the place where you trust yourself. Where your instincts matter more than other people's expectations. Where your signal is clear and strong and unmistakably *yours*.

This is your feral self, the one that never needed fixing. The one that remembered how to listen. The one that knows growth doesn't require **protection** or **performance**.

You're not trying to become anything anymore. You're here. Awake. Whole. And from here, everything is possible.

When you lead from wholeness, you don't just change systems. You heal them.

What You're Moving Toward

You already know this isn't an ending. It's a continuation…a widening circle. Not some final destination where you've got leadership figured out. You know better now. You're moving toward whatever comes next, knowing you can handle it without losing yourself in the process.

More challenges that require everything you've got. More opportunities to guide from your wholeness instead of your wounds. More moments when you get to choose presence over performance, substance over style, truth over comfort.

The work isn't getting easier. It's getting *more real*. The stakes aren't getting lower. They're getting clearer. The difference is you're not trying to be someone else anymore while you navigate complexity. You're just being yourself, which turns out to be exactly what the complexity needs.

You're not looking for approval anymore. You're choosing how to show up.

The trail ahead isn't marked. The challenges ahead aren't predictable. The people ahead aren't all going to like your approach.

None of that matters now. You know how to read what's emerging. You know how to trust what you're sensing. You know how to guide from your wholeness even when everyone around you is fragmenting.

Especially then.

Welcome back, guide. You've been here all along.

SIGNAL CHECK

SELF

What do you trust about yourself now that you used to second-guess, and how will that change your next decision?

TEAM

Where is your team already moving with the kind of trust and clarity you used to have to manufacture, and what becomes possible when you stop managing it and start following it?

CULTURE

What systems are you ready to design that make leading from wholeness the obvious choice?

About the Author

It's Good to See You Here

Linda Clark builds leaders who don't flinch.

For nearly three decades, she's worked at the intersection of strategy, organizational development, and human behavior, the place where trust either grows roots or burns out.

For the last ten years, she's focused on keynotes, executive coaching, and leadership development, impacting more than 25,000 leaders. She's the creator of the Curiosetti Method™ and firmly believes corporate trust falls should be a prosecutable offense.

The system failed leadership. We're building something better.

This is a method, a movement, a map.

On Stage

With more than 200 events in 10 years, conference organizers keep bringing Linda back for one reason: **she delivers stories, metaphors, and real talk that leave leaders laughing, squirming, and ready to act.**

She unpacks why urgency masquerades as importance, how strategy becomes a collective skill, and what happens when cultures drag like a tired mule (and kick!)

Her sessions leave leaders ready to have the hard conversations, redesign the broken systems, and lead differently starting Monday morning.

> "Strategy may set the pace, but culture decides if anyone keeps up."

Book her when you want substance that stays with people long after the applause.

The Work

As an executive coach, keynote speaker, and organizational strategist who helps leaders stop playing small and start building what lasts, Linda's approach blends surgical clarity, irreverent humor, and enough feral instinct to make the status quo nervous. She rewilds systems tamed by control into ones powered by curiosity and momentum.

From Fortune 100 boardrooms where politics stalled progress to founder-led startups running on caffeine and hope to nonprofits hanging on by a thread while trying to change the world, she's guided leaders through the messy, necessary work of building trust that doesn't crack when it counts.

She specializes in:

Leadership Development that produces guides who multiply capacity across teams, not managers with better vocabulary. The Curiosetti Method™ is modular, scalable, and built to rewild leadership back into something that works.

Executive Coaching that develops leaders who can handle complexity without losing themselves in it. Custom coaching and cohorts for leaders in the thick of it, rebuilding trust, sharpening clarity, and designing systems that flex instead of fracture.

Fractional Organizational Development for organizations where culture is on the line. Not a consultant with slides. A partner who sits at the table, names the hard truths, and builds systems that don't snap under pressure. Strategic, embedded, and built for high stakes.

Human Resources Transformation that addresses what's broken, not what looks good in the annual report. Building leadership pipelines that don't just fill seats but develop people who can navigate what's coming next.

She's designed and delivered programs for Oklahoma City University, Rose State College, and the University of Central Oklahoma. She's got a fancy resume of event appearances, has spent time as undergraduate professor of leadership, holds several credentials in the HR and coaching space, and values all of the experience over the years.

She works across sectors with one consistent goal: build systems wild enough to evolve and strong enough to stand.

Linda is a proud card-carrying member of The Curious, and plays in the intersection of being neurodivergent, queer, and human.

What People Say

"Her energy, insight, and ability to connect with our team left a lasting impact. The feedback was overwhelmingly positive." — Amy Downs, CEO

"Linda reframes the complex into clarity. Coaching with her changes everything." — Misty Babb-Hayes, CEO

Off the Clock

When she's not on stage or working with executive teams, you'll find her on big horses or running whitewater spicy enough to demand her ADHD play along.

Her writing and speaking connect leaders, HR professionals, organizational development practitioners, executive coaches, and curious professionals who want to build systems that thrive on change.

Want Linda to keynote your next event, develop your leadership team, or transform your organizational culture?

Text **FERAL to 66866** to connect or start the conversation at http://www.linda-clark.com

Choose Your Own Adventure

Guided Trails by Topic

You don't have to read this book in order. You're leading real work in real weather, and some days you only have time for a few miles. These trails help you start where the signal is strongest, trust, clarity, courage, belonging, and walk straight toward what needs your attention now. Pick a path, take what you find, and leave the trail better than you found it.

The Individual

Growth begins where awareness turns into skill. These trails strengthen the core competencies of curiosity, integrity, adaptability, and renewal. They build self-trust, creative range, and the discernment to move with clarity and courage.

- **Trust in Uncertain Times** Trust is steadiness made visible through consistent choices. The Curious rebuild it through presence, clarity, and follow-through.
  Reading Map: Chapter 2 · Chapter 1 · Chapter 8 · Chapter 10
  Begin with awareness. Restore confidence. Rebuild trust across the team. Realign what's true.

- **Integrity and Alignment** Integrity is leadership's quiet gravity. The Curious align motive, method, and meaning so clearly that others can orient by it.
  Reading Map: Chapter 2 · Chapter 4 · Chapter 10 · Chapter 11
  Notice drift early. Lead from your truest stance. Reconnect words and actions. Renew alignment through change.

- **Strategic Curiosity** Curiosity is strategy's first movement. The Curious use it to reveal unseen patterns and design smarter paths forward.

Reading Map: Chapter 2 · Chapter 6 · Chapter 5 · Chapter 7
Orient through questions. Explore complexity. Discover what's next.

- **Courage, Creativity, and Innovation** Courage acts from integrity when uncertainty is unavoidable. The Curious experiment boldly and stay whole in the process.
  Reading Map: Chapter 2 · Chapter 3 · Chapter 9 · Chapter 11
  Lead with curiosity. Show up as unrepeatable. Spark creative momentum. Sustain energy through renewal.

- **Hope and Renewal** Hope is direction with heartbeat. The Curious build it by naming what still works and moving from what's alive.
  Reading Map: Chapter 2 · Chapter 7 · Chapter 10 · Chapter 11
  Find orientation again. Restore belief. Reconnect for renewal. Turn resilience into rhythm.

- **Identity and Authentic Leadership** Authenticity is coherence you can feel. The Curious lead from identity that's lived, examined, and unperformed.
  Reading Map: Chapter 2 · Chapter 3 · Chapter 4 · Chapter 5 · Chapter 11
  Evolve awareness. Lead with bold honesty. Become who your work needs. Return to wholeness.

The Team

Teams become capable when connection turns into collaboration. These trails deepen the competencies that build collective strength, including communication, accountability, decision-making, and shared trust. They help teams align purpose with action, navigate tension, and sustain performance through change.

- **Signal and Clarity in Communication** Clarity is the shared understanding that lets a system breathe and act together. The Curious practice it by naming what matters without shrinking its complexity.
  Reading Map: Chapter 2 · Chapter 6 · Chapter 7
  See the signal. Accelerate decisions. Create shared direction

- **Collaboration and Collective Intelligence** Collaboration is disciplined listening in action. The Curious invite insight from the edges and turn it into shared direction.
  Reading Map: Chapter 2 · Chapter 6 · Chapter 7 · Chapter 8
  Map insight across boundaries. Think as a living system. Align through understanding. Practice trust together.

- **Conflict and Restoration** Restoration is conflict transformed into alignment. The Curious engage tension directly, using it to reveal priorities and build trust.
  Reading Map: Chapter 2 · Chapter 1 · Chapter 8 · Chapter 10
  Notice disruption early. Read tension for truth. Use disagreement as data. Repair through trust.

- **Being Trustworthy** Trustworthiness is reliability others can measure. The Curious demonstrate it through visible consistency and follow-through that sustains confidence.
  Reading Map: Chapter 2 · Chapter 1 · Chapter 8 · Chapter 10
  Start with self-honesty. Build credibility through consistency. Restore confidence. Live integrity daily.

- **Decision Making** Decision making is leadership's moment of proof. The Curious choose with clarity, act with courage, and adjust with humility.
  Reading Map: Chapter 2 · Chapter 6 · Chapter 7 · Chapter 9
  Perceive before choosing. Shape decisions through insight. Fuel clarity into motion. Act with courage in real time.

- **Accountability and Follow Through** Accountability is how trust learns it can stay. The Curious turn responsibility into rhythm and reliability others can depend on.
  Reading Map: Chapter 2 · Chapter 1 · Chapter 4 · Chapter 8
  Stay aware of impact. Repair through responsibility. Lead with integrity. Commit and complete.

The Culture

Culture matures when systems become self-aware. These trails grow the competencies that shape belonging, innovation, and sustainable impact. They invite leaders to think in ecosystems and design environments where inclusion, adaptability, and purpose thrive long after individual effort ends.

- **Belonging and Inclusion** Belonging is inclusion in motion. The Curious design systems where contribution changes outcomes and connection fuels trust.
  Reading Map: Chapter 2 · Chapter 5 · Chapter 8 · Chapter 10
  Locate yourself in the system. Root inclusion in every seed. Open belonging through design. Practice return through connection.

- **Systems Thinking** Systems thinking is awareness made operational. The Curious act from patterns, not panic, and design for interconnection rather than control.
  Reading Map: Chapter 2 · Chapter 6 · Chapter 10
  See the ecosystem. Think in ripple effects. Lead systems that live and adapt.

- **Adaptability and Change** Adaptability is practiced stability. The Curious read the current, adjust with awareness, and model steadiness in motion.
  Reading Map: Chapter 2 · Chapter 6 · Chapter 9
  Stay flexible without drift. Learn together. Create change through steady motion.

- **Purpose and Regeneration** Purpose is a renewable resource. The Curious align aspiration with design so that people, systems, and outcomes replenish one another.
  Reading Map: Chapter 2 · Chapter 4 · Chapter 7 · Chapter 10
  Orient toward meaning. Reclaim purpose through honesty. Renew commitment through clarity. Restore energy through design.

- **Purpose and Legacy**
  Legacy is purpose extended through systems. The Curious build structures that outlast personality and make impact sustainable across time.
  Reading Map: Chapter 2 · Chapter 4 · Chapter 7 · Chapter 11
  Lead from orientation. Build what lasts. Aim for long-view impact. Leave integrity as your echo.

www.ingramcontent.com/pod-product-compliance
Lightning Source LLC
Chambersburg PA
CBHW020541030426
42337CB00013B/927